HOW TO MAKE
PRAYER
MORE
EFFECTIVE

HERBERT LOCKYER

WHITAKER
HOUSE

All Scripture quotations are taken from the King James Version of the Holy Bible.

How to Make Prayer More Effective

ISBN: 978-1-60374-555-0

© 1953, 2012 by Ardis A. Lockyer

Whitaker House
1030 Hunt Valley Circle
New Kensington, PA 15068
www.whitakerhouse.com

PREFACE

When the invitation from the publishers reached me, asking that I write a book on prayer, I was somewhat diffident about such a task. Although I had been a Christian for almost half a century, I realized the need of tarrying longer in the school of prayer before writing about such a holy exercise. The more the proposition was prayerfully considered, however, the more I felt constrained to prepare a manual calculated to help the rank and file of Christian workers.

The reader will discern that no effort has been made to prove the reality of prayer. All the Bible does is state the fact of prayer and illustrate it with powerful examples of its reality. As Dr. William Evans expressed it, "Prayer does not need proof; it needs practice."

Without a doubt, prayer is the greatest art in the world—a holy art that needs only to be learned. If it is a lost art, it is lost only because man has lost the consciousness of God. Dr. Ole Hallesby, whose great book *Prayer* is widely known, said,

> Prayer is a fine, delicate instrument. To use it right is a great art, a holy art. There is perhaps no greater art than the art of prayer. The other fine arts require a great deal of native ability, much knowledge, and a great deal of money to cover the cost of a long and expensive period of training. Fortunately, such is not the case with the art of prayer.
>
> It requires neither great native ability, nor much knowledge, nor money. The least gifted, the uneducated, and the poor can cultivate the holy art of prayer. However,

certain requirements must also be met, if the art of prayer is to be acquired. In the main, they are two: practice and perseverance.

The conspicuous weakness in present-day Christianity is the lack of an effective prayer ministry. Toyohiko Kagawa, addressing second-generation Japanese Christians on the West Coast, said, "Your greatest lack is that you do not know how to pray." Each of us must confess that our Christian life is so anemic and ineffective because we have not learned the art and the discipline of prayer. "The disparity between the prayer-privilege as seen in God's Word, and the prayer-practice as seen in daily life," as Dr. Norman Harrison put it, should be a matter of concern to those who desire a Spirit-inspired witness. The difference between Christians can be traced to their conception of prayer. He who does not pray is not, and cannot be, a Christian after the New Testament order— nor has the Christian who does not pray *habitually* more than a miserable foundation for a hope.

The holiest and most fruitful soulwinners are those who make much of prayer. The greatest preachers of the gospel and missionaries of the cross are those who come most often, and linger longest, at the mercy seat of prayer. As we shall presently see, the Bible saints had a unique sense of the presence of God. To them, heaven was not far from earth. They treated prayer as an attitude of life, not as a series of isolated acts. They viewed prayer as a necessity and, as William E. Gladstone put it, "the highest expression of the human intellect." For them, prayer was able to bend the arm of God.

It is never easy to pray! It may seem easy, yet nothing is more difficult. Prayer has been described as "the strangest adventure in human life." Without spiritual and mental and physical effort, one can repeat a written prayer; but to pray in the Spirit, to experience a heart cry ascending to heaven, involves pain, planning, and perseverance. The purpose, then, of our study of the nature of prayer is to set forth the simplicity and effectiveness of heartfelt communication with God.

The Westminster Shorter Catechism has beautifully and clearly expressed the full idea of prayer in these words: "Prayer is an offering up of our desires unto God, for things agreeable to His will, in the name of Christ, with confession of our sins, and thankful acknowledgment of His mercies." Therefore, prayer may be broken down as:

1. An offering up of our desires

2. Unto God

3. For things agreeable to His will

4. In the name of Christ

5. With confession of our sins, and

6. Thankful acknowledgment of His mercies.

The writer feels that his labor will not have been in vain if one soul, with a deep desire to pray, gathers guidance, instruction, and inspiration from the pages that follow. It is with sincere gratitude that he records his indebtedness to help received from books, booklets, and articles on prayer, many of which are mentioned at the end of his book in a section entitled "Prayer Guides to Follow."

—Dr. Herbert Lockyer

CONTENTS

CHAPTER 1

THE ANTIQUITY OF PRAYER

Prayer is as old as the human race. We cannot conceive of God creating Adam and Eve without implanting within them the desire and the ability to converse with their Creator. The sacred narrative reveals that our first parents communed with God. The morning stars were not alone in their songs of praise over a newborn world. Naturally, and instinctively, Adam and Eve would lift their voices in homage and praise to their Maker. Even when their disobedience resulted in expulsion from the garden of Eden, we can imagine how they would have asked for pardoning mercy at the hand of the Lord. They talked with Him; and what is prayer, in its simplest form, but man's innate instinct to talk to God?

Prayer, then, is the oldest and most universal of all religious exercises. Men began from the earliest ages to call upon the name of the Lord. Some say that the Greeks called man *anthropos* because he is the being with its face upturned toward God. Man was born to pray. He has been styled "a praying animal," "a praying being." Man will pray, whether it be to the true God or to an idol of his own creation. Prayer is a dictate of nature, "a constitutional instinct inwrought by the Maker," as James Barr Walker described it. It is natural and instinctive for man to call upon a being greater than himself to aid him in time of need. This is why the most godless cry out to God when cast into sudden and extreme peril. There is, in the nature of man, or in the circumstances in which he is conditioned, something that leads him to recognize and worship a superior being. Man is a religious being; he will worship.

Prayer, then, is a reality; it is supremely natural to man. There are some who argue that prayer is mere assumption. Others speak of it as superstition, or an unmanly habit of weaklings in time of panic. But men in all ages have prayed. They never outgrow prayer. Any disbelief in its reality resides in the opinions, not the impulses, of men. Prayer is the native impulse of the soul. Its custom is as old as human awe, and it takes countless moods and forms. As the ancient Egyptians used to bully their gods, so the Australian aborigine carried a severed hand, to which he would say, "Guide me right, or I throw you to the dogs." Muslims prostrate themselves on a rug; Tibetan Buddhists write their supplications on tiny flags and stick them in a mound for the wind to carry away; Catholics finger their rosaries; Quakers sit together in silence. From every corner of the world, at every hour of the day and night, to one God or another, rise the prayers or meditations of religious beings. In the majority of cases, unbiblical prayers are never directly and literally answered, yet men and women pray on.

For a fuller treatment of the universality of prayer, the reader is directed to the chapter entitled "Non-Christian Prayer and Missions" in Samuel Zwemer's *Taking Hold of God*. In striking fashion, Dr. Zwemer proves that there is no tribe or people, however degraded or ignorant of even the beginnings of civilization, that does not pray: "Men began to pray and continued to pray, because the necessity of their moral nature bade them commune with the unseen."

> Far and wide, though all unknowing,
> Pants for Thee each mortal breast,
> Human tears for Thee are flowing,
> Human hearts in Thee would rest.[1]

Somehow, man feels that he belongs to two worlds, and that prayer is the ladder by which he can climb from the one world

---

1. Arthur C. Coxe, "Savior, Sprinkle Many Nations," 1851.

to the other. The following are a few condensed facts from Dr. Zwemer's great work.

The ancient Greeks prayed in short formulas, which they believed had magical powers. Plato said, "Every man of sense before beginning any important work will ask help of the gods." Friedrich Heiler, in a study on prayer as a universal element in all early religions, devoted one hundred pages to the prayers and prayer customs of primitive tribes in Africa, Australia, and North America. A study of the prayer life of pagan tribes reveals a special reverence and an attitude of awe in the worshippers as they approached the unseen Spirit, whose dwelling place was high above men and whose attributes were not like those of mortals.

As a rule, primitive prayers were on a low plane and, in respect to non-Christians, were offered in the outer court of the temple. Theirs was not the boldness to enter in to the holiest of all. Their prayers were for temporal blessings and successes. Good crops, rain, healing, peace from war—these formed the burden of heathen cries.

Prayer, then, is bound up with the basic beliefs of life. Man, as a religious being, recognizes that prayer is the breath of his life, the most divine exercise the heart can engage in. Man, as part of God's creation, has a nature that cries out for God. As St. Augustine wrote in his *Confessions*, "Thou hast made us for Thyself, and our hearts are restless till they find their rest in Thee." Prayer is the answer to the soul's clamant hunger for God. It is the evidence of an unseen divine power outside one's self.

In succeeding chapters, we hope to prove that prayer is a working force in Christian experience, and that Christians pray, and persist in prayer, because of prayer's efficacy. The saints of all ages have prayed, not out of sentiment, or because they thought prayer was simply an instinct. They have proven that prayer is not a presumption, but that it works miracles in human lives. "Who rises from prayer a better man," said George Meredith, "his prayer is answered." This force of prayer makes saints. As E. M. Bounds expressed it, "Holy characters are formed by the power of real praying. The more of true saints, the more of praying; the more of praying, the more of true saints." We do not bow down to idols of stone and wood that have ears but hear not. We have the full revelation of God as One who can be approached directly through Christ, by the Spirit, and who, loving to hear His children pray, is ever ready to answer Spirit-inspired prayers.

A full recognition of the privilege of approaching God will save us from any irreverence, undue familiarity, or unpreparedness as we enter the presence of God. Social barriers often keep us from conversing with the noble of the land. Before Esther could speak to King Ahasuerus, she had to wait for the waving of the golden scepter in her direction. (See Esther 5:2; 8:4.)

CHAPTER 2

THE PRIVILEGE OF PRAYER

Although we often sing about the privilege of carrying everything to God in prayer, must we not confess that familiarity of approach has the tendency to make us forget that prayer is a privilege? Who are we that we should be able to take God's name upon our lips and tell Him all that is upon our hearts? He is high and holy, the Lord God Almighty, yet here are we, mere worms of earth, with authority to come before God at any time, in any place, and commune with Him! How different with ourselves! We have not to wait upon any whim or movement of God, nor for the office of any human intermediary priest. No matter who we are or where we are, by grace, we have the right to come immediately into the presence of Him who bids His children ask and receive.

William Wallace Horner reminds us that "among the callings and privileges accorded to God's children, prayer holds the supreme place, and is of inestimable value both to the prayer and to those for whom he prays."

Our common tragedy is that of failure to take advantage of such a priceless privilege. We are not victorious in life and fruitful in service, all because the communication line with heaven is not in constant use. Privileged with daily opportunities of dwelling with the King and appropriating all His wealth of power and wisdom, we yet live as those who delight in penury.

Old Testament saints understood something of the privilege of taking hold on God. But under the old economy, God localized His presence in the temple, and the Jew had to come thither to pray. Under grace, the spirit, and not the mere sphere, of worship is all-important. (See John 4:24.) The child of God can draw nigh anywhere. Such is his higher privilege, that, through Christ, he can converse with Him in barn or cathedral. God is no respecter of places. And, as the hymn "What a Friend We Have in Jesus" reminds us, we forfeit much peace of mind, all because we fail to take full advantage of the blessed, exalted privileges of prayer.

Our conception of the privilege of prayer also determines the manner of our approach to God. If the fact is never lost sight of that it is most condescending on the part of *"the King eternal, immortal, invisible, the only wise God"* (1 Timothy 1:17) to offer us immediate access into His presence, then all due reverence and humility will be ours. When the Jews of old came before Him, they bowed their heads and worshipped. As the seraphim waited before Him, they veiled their faces and acclaimed Him as the thrice-holy Lord God Almighty. (See Isaiah 6:2–3.)

C. S. Lewis spoke of those whose conception of God is "the God we have done a corner in"; the sort who seem to think of themselves as more "pally" with God than others! But how dare we be unduly familiar with Him before whom the whole court of heaven bows in willing submission?

> O how shall I, whose native sphere
> Is dark, whose mind is dim,
> Before the Ineffable appear?[2]

A scriptural understanding of the privilege of prayer likewise prevents us from treating God as, more or less, One who is on our own level—One with whom we can barter and selfishly petition, "Tell You what I'll do, God. Let's make a deal: You give me this, and I'll do that." No, no. Such an attitude is the abuse of

---

2. Thomas Binney, "Eternal Light! Eternal Light!" c. 1826.

our privilege; it is the survival of the primitive sacrifice, an offer to trade incense for luck.

The words *"boldness"* and *"confidence,"* used in connection with prayer in Ephesians 3:12 and Hebrews 4:5, 19–22 to signify freedom of speech or the liberty to ask anything, sufficiently indicate the inestimable privilege of prayer, but they in no way indicate license or flippant familiarity. (See Psalm 89:17.) The appealing words of Montgomery should ever be in mind:

> Lord, teach us how to pray aright,
> With reverence and with fear;
> Though dust and ashes in Thy sight,
> We may, we must draw near.
> Give deep humility; the sense
> Of godly sorrow give;
> A strong, desiring confidence
> To hear Thy voice, and live.[3]

Prayer is heaven's telephone, which is free to all, always disengaged, and never out of order. The line, however, is always used with reverence and godly fear.

---

3. James Montgomery, "Lord, Teach Us How to Pray Aright," 1818.

CHAPTER 3

THE NATURE OF PRAYER

What exactly is prayer? It is the most universal and the most intense expression of God-given instincts, yet it is, of "all the acts and states of the soul, the most difficult to define," says Samuel Zwemer. "It escapes definition, and is broader, higher, deeper than all human language."

A short while ago, the writer heard a gifted Bible expositor, the author of a helpful book on prayer, affirm that prayer is asking—nothing more, or less, than asking. But is this so? Certainly, asking is an integral part of prayer, for the root idea of "to pray" is "to ask." But surely, asking is only one form, although a vital and essential part, of the soul's approach to God.

Old Testament Hebrew words for prayer suggest intercession or intervention, with a root connection to words meaning "to judge" and "to entreat." Coming to the New Testament, we find the general Greek word translated for prayer is *proseuche*, which is a compound word—*pros*, suggesting direction towards, and *euche*, standing for the simple prayer or vow. In the majority of cases, the term simply indicates the activity of the prayer toward God.

Another word used by the New Testament writers is *deomai*—"to ask or beg for," from the root *deo*—"to want or need." Still another term is *erotao*—"to question, to ask," employed by Christ in John 14:16. Other words are *aiteo*—"to ask, beg, call for," and *enteuxis*—"intercession," used for *"prayer"* in 1 Timothy 4:5. Paul gave us four different words, all related to prayer, in one verse: "*I exhort therefore, that, first of all, **supplications, prayers, intercessions,*** *and giving of thanks, be made for all men*" (1 Timothy 2:1, emphasis added). Here we have *deesis* (from *deomai*), "the need...want... seeking"; *proseuche*, "prayer addressed to God"; *enteuxis*, "meeting with"; and *eucharistia*, from which we have the word *eucharist*, a word meaning "thankfulness." The Latin word for prayer is *precaria*, from which *precarious* comes, implies something to be obtained by begging or entreaty.

When the disciples, seeing Jesus at prayer, presented their request, "*Lord, teach us to pray*" (Luke 11:1), He did not reply, "Prayer is simply asking God for what you want." He gave them the model prayer, which we call the Lord's Prayer (see Luke 11:2–4), in which asking God for what we want forms but a minor part. Two-thirds of this prayer is taken up with worship, adoration, and praise.

It would seem as if our Lord condemns too much asking in His discourse, since He reminded His disciples that their heavenly Father already knew of their creaturely needs. (See Matthew 6:8.) If this is true, and it is, then why devote so much breath in begging God for those things He knows we have need of? A mystic of the sixteenth century reminds us that "prayer is to ask not what we wish of God, but what God wishes of us."

What we call prayer is many-sided. It is referred to in Scripture as request, incense, intercession, entreaty, complaint, meditation, supplication, waiting, etc. According to the Franciscan pattern, there are eight steps in prayer: recollection, contrition, devotion, reading, meditation, thanksgiving, oblation (or consecration), and petition.

Matthew Henry, the great Bible commentator, gave these five parts of prayer: adoration, confession, petition, thanksgiving, and intercession. Norman Harrison observed, "Prayer is not of an unvarying uniformity in its expression, but rather falls naturally into different phases, or parts, according to the prevailing purpose in view. Our approach to God the Father calls for adoration and worship. Our use of 'the name' leads on to petition and intercession. And the needful accompaniments of prayer call for confession and thanksgiving." Truly, there are many facets to the diamond of prayer.

Karl Sabiers summarized the different standpoints of prayer in this telling fashion:

1. The praying which is worship, adoration, and communion, without any thought of asking for anything

2. The praying and asking we do for ourselves, to get the will of God into our own lives

3. The praying we do for others, that the will of God may be done in their lives

Prayer is, first and foremost, an act of homage from the creature to the Creator, the highest expression of our allegiance to Him, and, thus,, a precious privilege and a binding duty. No matter what phase of prayer we may think of, the very act implies the existence of a Person greater than ourselves. We cannot ask anything from a wall or an influence. If there is no personal God, then prayer is empty and valueless.

Prayer, then, is not to be regarded as a means of getting what we want from God—not merely that. It is the method by which we give unto the Lord the glory due His name. It involves the highest exercise of adoration of which the human spirit is capable. Then, there is also devout meditation, or the listening side of prayer. (See Numbers 7:89.) Longfellow must have had this aspect of prayer before him when he wrote these expressive lines:

> Let us, then, labour for an inward stillness—
> An inward stillness and an inward healing,
> That perfect silence where the lips and heart
> Are still, and we no longer entertain

Our own imperfect thoughts and vain opinions,
But God alone speaks in us, and we wait
In singleness of heart, that we may know
His will, and in the silence of our spirits,
That we may do His will, and do that only.

It is profitable to gather together many of the defini-
tions writers have used to describe the nature of prayer. James
Montgomery, in his great prayer hymn, gave us fourteen aspects
in six stanzas.

Prayer is the soul's sincere desire,
Uttered or unexpressed,
The motion of a hidden fire
That trembles in the breast.

Prayer is the burden of a sigh,
The falling of a tear,
The upward glancing of an eye
When none but God is near.

Prayer is the simplest form of speech
That infant lips can try;
Prayer the sublimest strains that reach
The majesty on high.

Prayer is the contrite sinner's voice
Returning from his ways,
While angels in their songs rejoice,
And cry: Behold, he prays!

Prayer is the Christian's vital breath,
The Christian's native air,
His watchword at the gates of death;
He enters heaven with prayer.

> O Thou by whom we come to God,
> The Life, the Truth, the Way!
> The path of prayer Thyself hast trod;
> Lord! Teach us how to pray. [4]

Other authors have spoken of prayer as "the passage from spiritual thirst to spiritual refreshing." "If prayer is anything, it is everything; if it is truth, it is the greatest truth." "Prayer is a dialogue, not a monologue; it is a vision as well as a voice; it is a revelation as well as a supplication." "Prayer is not a mere venture and a voice of mine, but a vision and a voice divine." "Prayer," said John Bunyan, "is a sincere, sensible journey out of the soul to God, through Christ, and in the strength and assistance of the Holy Spirit, for such things as God has promised."

Isaiah gave us a definition of prayer surpassing all others in boldness, simplicity, and psychological accuracy: "*There is none that calleth upon thy name, that stirreth up himself to take hold of thee*" (Isaiah 64:7). The literal Hebrew, said Samuel Zwemer, implies that to pray is to rouse oneself out of sleep and to seize hold of Jehovah; it implies the pathos of a suppliant who is in deadly earnest—the arms, the hands, the very fingers of the soul reaching out to lay hold of God, man's personal, spiritual appropriation of Deity.

According to Zwemer, prayer is "the highest exercise of the affections, the will, the memory, the imagination, and the conscience." He also said that "daily prayer is the gymnasium of the soul."

We cannot do better than to close this section of our meditation with the weighty words of Ole Hallesby, who, in describing the nature of prayer, wrote, "Prayer life has its own laws, as all the rest of life has. The fundamental law in prayer is this: Prayer is given and ordained for the purpose of glorifying God. Prayer is

---

4. James Montgomery, "Prayer is the Soul's Sincere Desire," 1818.

the appointed way of giving Jesus an opportunity to exercise His supernatural powers of salvation. And in so doing He desires to make use of us."[5]

Is this our conception of prayer? Understanding its true nature, are we proving that it is the God-given way by which our lean souls can be restored to spiritual health and vigor? Are we proving that all the emotions of the soul can be exercised in the right way, through the employment of the lost art of secret prayer?

5. Ole Hallesby, *Prayer* (Minneapolis, MN: Augsburg Publishing House, 1931), 129.

CHAPTER 4

THE PHILOSOPHY OF PRAYER

Closely associated with the nature of intercourse with God is a philosophy we must master if we are to know how to pray effectually. Prayer is well nigh impossible without a primary conviction, namely, that there is a living, personal, intelligent God to whom we can pray and with whom we can freely communicate. Accepting such a premise, the question "Why pray?" becomes rather "Why not pray?" Belief in God makes prayer a self-justifying achievement.

The very quintessence of the philosophy of prayer is asking God in faith for what we need, or, rather, for what He wants us to have. The deist argues that God is too transcendent, too far above man, to be expected to listen to man's prayers. But the Bible affirms that He is not too remote, or man too insignificant, for prayer to be a vital transaction between God and creation. At the heart of prayer, there is a lively sense of God's unremitting care for His people. A God who does not care does not count! Augustine cried, "O Thou Good Omnipotent, who so carest for every one of us, as if Thou carest for him alone; and so for all, as if all were but one!"

God is likewise omniscient. He sees all and each in all. We appear to be lost in a crowd, but we are not so to God. "*Thou God seest me*" (Genesis 16:13). The psalmist declared that God knows the stars by name. (See Psalm 147:4.) Our Lord told us that He knows His own by name. (See John 10:3.) Thus, prayer becomes real to us as we experience that personal appropriation of faith in God's care for each one of us.

To assure our souls of God's care, all we have to do is to turn to the Psalms. How real God was to the saints of old! They had no doubt as to the true import of prayer. Think of Psalm 31, where the writer went to God in the confidence that He was a strong rock and fortress. (See Psalm 31:2–3.) Men had forgotten the writer and destroyed his trust in them, but he triumphantly declared, "*I trust in the* LORD" (verse 6).

Wrapped in the philosophy of prayer is the fact at which we have already hinted: that prayer has its laws. If we disregard these laws, or act contrary to the idea and essence of prayer, how can we pray aright? Sound, normal, effective prayer can be ours only as we respect and obey God's laws that govern prayer. According to William Wallace Horner, there are four things that are superlatively essential: righteous living, faith in God, the guidance of the Holy Spirit, and the will of God.

We all possess the "noble capacity for prayer," but it becomes a vital force in our lives only when we turn to God in perfect simplicity and naturalness, knowing that He knows, He loves, and He cares. George Müller, that mighty man of prayer, who trusted God implicitly for his orphans, has given us his idea of the philosophy of prayer in this unforgettable way:

1. "I seek at the beginning to get my heart into such a state that it has no will of its own in regard to a given matter. Nine-tenths of the trouble with people generally is at this point. Nine-tenths of the difficulties are overcome when our hearts are ready to do the Lord's will, whatever it may be. When one is truly in this state, it is usually but a little way before one discovers the knowledge of what God's will is.

2. "Having done this, I do not leave the result to feeling or simple impression. If so, I make myself liable to great delusions.

3. "I seek the will of the Spirit of God through, or in connection with, the Word of God. The Spirit and the Word must be combined. If I look to the Spirit alone without the Word, I also lay myself open to great delusions. If the Holy Spirit

guides us at all, He will do it according to the Scriptures and never contrary to them.

4. "Next, I take into account providential circumstances. These often plainly indicate God's will in connection with His Word and Spirit.

5. "I ask God in prayer to reveal His will to me so that I may understand it correctly.

6. "Thus, through prayer to God, the study of the Word, and reflection, I come to a deliberate judgment according to the best of my ability and knowledge, and if my mind is thus at peace, and continues so after two or three more petitions, I proceed accordingly."[6]

In his heart-stirring volume *Quiet Talks on Prayer*, S. D. Gordon laid down the philosophy of prayer in these clear-cut lines:

1. There must be an understanding—a working agreement, a fixed, invariable hour of prayer activeness.

2. There must be a time and a place spent in communication in accord with working agreement.

3. Sooner or later, the known results will come.

Then, Dr. Gordon asked, "The Law of Prayer Action—what is it?" He answered his question in this forceful way:

1. Prayer must be in Jesus' name.

2. Prayer must be by a person in full touch with Jesus—in heart, habit, and life.

3. Prayer must be in harmony with the teachings of the Bible.

4. Prayer must be actual, simple, definite, and confident—"in faith believing."

---

6. George Müller, *Answers to Prayer* (edited from George Muller's narratives by A. E. C. Brooks in 1896. Chicago: The Moody Press, 1896), 2.

'Tis not enough to bend the knee,
And words of prayer to say,
The heart must with the lips agree,
Or else we do not pray.[7]
For words, without the heart
The Lord will never hear;
Nor will He to those lips attend
Whose prayers are not sincere.[8]

---

7. E. M. Bounds, *The Essentials of Prayer* (New Kensington, PA: Whitaker House, 1991), 13.
8. John Burton, "I Often Say My Prayers, But Do I Ever Pray?" 1860.

CHAPTER 5

THE NECESSITY OF PRAYER

Prayer is not only an instinct and a privilege but also a divine and human imperative. Jesus reminded His own of the necessity of prayer in the words, *"Men ought always to pray"* (Luke 18:1). "We will never pray as we should until we see it as a necessity," said Norman Harrison, "indispensable to the life we have undertaken to live." Then, this gifted brother went on to state seven outstanding reasons for prayer's necessity:

1. To honor God as our Father (see Matthew 7:7–11)

2. To discharge our office as priests (see 1 Peter 2:5, 9)

3. To avail ourselves of our new privilege as believers (see John 16:24)

4. To fulfill our obligation to fellow believers (see Ephesians 6:18)

5. To seek and to save the souls of men (see 1 Timothy 2:4)

6. To outwit and overcome the powers of evil (see Ephesians 6:1, 12; 1 Peter 5:8–9)

7. To grow personally in grace and godliness (see 1 Timothy 4:7; 2 Peter 3:18)

Prayer is as necessary to our spiritual well-being as fresh air is to our physical welfare. Perhaps it was this thought that led James Montgomery to speak of prayer as "the Christian's vital breath, the Christian's native air."

We not only grieve the Lord; we also injure our own souls when we *"restrainest prayer before God"* (Job 15:4). Even when we are not engaged directly in public or family worship, it is necessary to live in unbroken contact with heaven.

Furthermore, nothing can be obtained from God without prayer. While all that is needful and beneficial has been divinely promised, prayer is essential if promises are to be realized in our experience. *"I will yet for this be enquired of by the house of Israel, to do it for them"* (Ezekiel 36:37).

William Proctor reminds us that "the necessity of prayer is evident from what is recorded of its results in the individual and corporate life of the early church, as compared with those in the modern church.... We have better organization, sounder scholarship, and more eloquent preaching, but we have less fervent individual prayer—and earnest, united intercession."

The book of Acts, so full of prayer, proves this point. To the apostles, there could not be any power for holy service apart from intercourse with God.

Christ ever recognized His need of prayer. What utter dependence upon the Father He manifested! To Him, prayer was no pleasant, hurried pastime but an agony of desire. Strong crying and tears accompanied His supplications. Writing for preachers, E. M. Bounds said, "Prayer is not a little habit pinned on to us while we were tied to our mothers' apron-strings, neither is it a little decent quarter-of-a-minute's grace said over an hour's dinner, but it is a most serious work of our most serious years.... Light praying will make light preaching." To that, we can add *light living.*

In *The Pilgrim's Progress,* how does John Bunyan's Christian, walking through the valley of the shadow of death on that narrow pathway between the quagmire and the pit, with horrible creeping things around his feet and foul fiends hissing in his ears, face his peril? Christian casts aside his sword and takes to himself the weapon of prayer. In this picture Bunyan gives us of the soul fighting foes without and within, there is a forceful lesson for our hearts to learn. To us, as good soldiers of Jesus Christ, prayer is our most necessary and effective weapon against the world, the flesh, and the devil. Christ won His victory in prayer before He appeared on the battlefield of action. (See Matthew 4:1–11.)

Prayer, as a spiritual weapon, acts in a twofold way: as a weapon of defense and as a weapon of offense.

PRAYER AS A WEAPON OF DEFENSE

By prayer, we can claim protection for the body against weakness, disease, or accident; for the mind against deceit, delusion, and discouragement; for the spirit against bad moods, jealousy, hardness; and for the will against paralyzing fear or crippling indecision. Defense for any phase of life can be claimed by prayer.

Daniel, threatened with death because of a demand to recall a dream of the king and to reveal its content, faced a humanly impossible situation by prayer. (See Daniel 2:14–23.) He wanted to know God's plans; praying, he received an answer. (See Daniel 9.) Later, he was troubled, and for three weeks, he fasted and prayed. Satanic forces resisted his efforts (see Daniel 10:12–14), but, ultimately, Daniel prevailed.

PRAYER AS A WEAPON OF OFFENSE

Often, secret prayer is related to public action. Waiting upon God, we get our plan of attack. Prayer is vision, unfolding God's purpose for life and service. Prayer is also the secret of inspiration. Strength, courage, and endurance become ours to fulfill the divine purpose as we pray. Meditate upon the great fighting prayers of the Bible: of Asa (see 2 Chronicles 14:11), of Jehoshaphat (see 2 Chronicles 20:6–13), of Hezekiah (see Isaiah 37:14–20), and of Nehemiah (see Nehemiah 4:9).

Principalities and powers,
Mustering their unseen array,
Wait for thy unguarded hours;
"Watch and pray."[9]

Man is helpless apart from prayer. His very presence before God is an evidence of his inability to do anything unless divine aid is forthcoming. "Prayer and helplessness are inseparable," E. M. Bounds reminds us. The more conscious we are of our utter inability and weakness, the greater the intensity of our prayers. Looking into the face of God, our own vaunted wisdom and fancied strength quickly disappear. Ole Hallesby wrote, "Only he who is helpless can truly pray."

Too many of us have a weak prayer life simply because we are puffed up with our own self-knowledge, self-sufficiency, and self-ability. We know it all; we can do it all; so why pray? But apart from Christ, we are nothing and can do nothing. (See Philippians 4:13). The poet Hartley Coleridge well stated,

Be not afraid to pray—to pray is right.
Pray, if thou canst, with hope; but ever pray,
Though hope be weak, or sick with long delay;
Pray in the darkness, if there be no light.

---

9. Charlotte Elliott, "Christian! Seek Not Yet Repose," 1836.

CHAPTER 6

THE FOUNDATION OF PRAYER

While reaching God is the chief objective in prayer, it must be recognized that He will hear us only as we approach Him in divinely appointed ways. Prayer is futile unless we come to God as He directs. And because of the importance of prayer, God tells us how He functions as the Hearer and the Answerer of prayer. All within the blessed Trinity are involved:

1. God the Father promises to heed the cry of His own;

2. God the Son, by His sacrificial death, provided an access into the holiest of all, and, through His resurrection and ascension, He has taken His place as our great High Priest to respond to those prayers offered in His name;

3. God the Spirit incites true prayer. We know not how to pray aright, but He helps such an infirmity.

Thus, the triune God is associated with our petitions, which are ever effective when we come to God, through Christ, by the Spirit.

Chief among the foundational principles of prayer is the right use of the name of Christ. If prayer is to be acceptable, it must be offered in His name. (See John 14:13–14; 15:16.) To use the name of another instead of our own is to deny ourselves and identify ourselves with the friend's name we present. This represents a tie between two persons.

Using the name of Christ does not mean that we lightly and mechanically append it to our prayers, as we might tie a label to a parcel. Asking in Christ's name is more than a customary formula; it involves correspondence with His will and harmony with His wishes. (See Acts 19:13–16.)

Just as there is a Dead Letter Office, there is also a Dead Prayer Office. Many of our prayers miss their way because they are wrongly addressed. Jesus said, *"No man cometh unto the Father, but by me"* (John 14:6, emphasis added). Therefore, no matter how religious a person may appear to be, if he denies the mediation and advocacy of Christ and approaches God in a way of his own choosing, his prayers are dead. Apart from Christ, we are spiritually bankrupt, having nothing to our credit. Coming to our bountiful Father above for help, we must draw and present our checks in the only name honored in heaven's bank: the peerless name of Jesus.

Another clear-cut direction for acceptable prayer is that it must be in full accord with the will of God. (See 1 John 5:14–15.) Too often, our prayers project our own will and wishes. Jesus could pray, *"Not my will, but thine, be done"* (Luke 22:42). As we shall later see, there is one reason we experience unanswered prayer: prayers stained with petulant self-will merit no answer.

> Not what we wish, but what we want,
> O let Thy grace supply;
> The good, unmasked, in mercy grant;
> The ill, though asked, deny.[10]

Another key to prayer response is the recognition of the Holy Spirit as "the Guide of prayer, and the Guarantor of its success." The clearer revelation of prayer in the New Testament stresses the role played by the Holy Spirit in our intercession (see Romans 8:26; Ephesians 2:18; Jude 20), as we shall discover when we come to chapter 13, "The Inspirer of Prayer."

---

10. James Merrick, "Eternal God, We Look to Thee," 1763.

Inherent in the relationship existing between God and man is the indispensable condition of faith for the granting of requests: *"If you have faith, and doubt not"* (Matthew 21:21). Faith is the means of communication with the invisible God and is essential to the offering and answering of prayer. (See Hebrews 11:6; James 1:6–7.) "Many of our prayers fail to enter heaven," says William Proctor, "for the same reason that a whole generation of Israelites failed to enter Canaan, 'because of unbelief.'" (See Hebrews 3:18–19; Matthew 17:19–21.)

There is a vital connection between prayer and faith. To quote Proctor again, "Faith is prayer in the heart, and prayer is faith on the lips.... Prayer is the key to all the treasures of divine grace; it opens all the doors and gives access to all the stores; but faith is the hand that uses the key." No matter how great the petition presented, "Faith," as Charles Wesley stated, "looks to God alone, laughs at impossibilities, and cries, 'It shall be done.'"

At the foundation of all prayer must be that absolute reliance upon the promises of God. (See 2 Samuel 7:28–29). What God has promised, He is able to perform, and we prayerfully appropriate His promises. The precious promises of God are both our warrant for praying and our security for receiving. We have no authority for asking anything beyond the all-embracing scope of the exceedingly great promises covering all our needs for body, soul, and spirit. (See 2 Peter 1:4; 2 Corinthians 1:20.)

No saint need have any doubt about the fulfillment of any divine promise, since a divine promise rests upon three great and glorious facts:

1. THE TRUTH OF GOD

He cannot deny Himself. He is not a man that He should lie. He must be true to His own character. (See Numbers 23:19; Hebrews 6:18.)

2. THE LOVE OF GOD

Earthly love can forget a promise, but God's perfect love will not suffer Him to forget all He has promised on our behalf. (See Isaiah 44:21; 49:15.)

3. THE POWER OF GOD

Because He is Almighty, He has the ability to perform all He has promised. Not one word can fail. (See Genesis 18:14; Luke 1:37.)

Another secret of effectual prayer is "a life inwardly right and outwardly upright," to use Norman Harrison's telling phrase. Prayer and purity are partners. It is as we live that we pray; it is the life that prays. It is not what we try to be when praying, but what we are when not praying, that gives power to our prayer life. Inconsistency of any kind prevents answers to our prayers. It is sadly possible to be indifferent regarding the claim of God upon our lives yet to run to Him in every emergency.

He is only a makeshift in a time of crisis. What a mean action! Unless we pray with holy hearts and hands, God refuses to hear. (See Psalm 66:18.) Unless we pray without wrath, God is silenced by our injury of a brother. (See Mark 11:25.) Let us therefore heed the advice of C. H. Spurgeon to "prepare our prayers by preparing ourselves." (See 1 John 3:22.) The whole man should be one burning prayer.

D. M. Panton, discussing the foundational form of prayer, said,

1. It should be *brief*. (See Ecclesiastes 5:2.) One stone flung hard is better than a handful of gravel, loose.

2. It should be *humble* (see Luke 18:13), for pride is Satan's wedge for splitting prayer meetings to pieces.

3. It should be *pointed*. (See Philippians 4:6.) Every prayer should be full of pointed phrases and definite petitions.

4. It should be *scriptural*. (See Luke 11:1.) To pray scripturally is a safe way to pray according to the will of God.

5. It should be offered *in faith* and *with gratitude*. (See James 1:7.) Faith and thankfulness are the wings of prayer (see 1 Thessalonians 5:18), which lift it readily to the throne.

6. It should be *intense*. (See Deuteronomy 4:29.) Satan can build walls around us but no roof overhead; but we may add that lethargy—and mere liturgy—build a ceiling to our prayers.

Satan is out to block our prayers. He is an obstinate and determined foe and fighter, and he has the accumulated wisdom of thousands of years when it comes to strategy. When the believer is on true praying ground, he is the target of satanic antagonism and can be victorious over the wiles of the enemy only as he continuously pleads the name and the blood of the Redeemer. In the prayer conflict, Calvary gives the child of God vantage ground. *"They overcame him* [the devil, the accuser] *by the blood of the Lamb"* (Revelation 12:11).

> Gird thine heavenly armor on,
> Wear it ever night and day;
> Ambushed lies the evil one;
> "Watch and pray!"[11]

---

11. Elliott, "Christian! Seek Not Yet Repose."

THE HABITS AND HABITAT
OF PRAYER

Because prayer is both an art and an attitude, there are one or two aspects of the theme which, while they do not touch the essentials of prayer, still call for consideration. Let us see if we can gather some practical and profitable suggestions from Scripture, as well as from the spiritual experiences of the saints of God through the ages, regarding the habits and habitat of prayer.

THE PLACE OF PRAYER

The *sphere* of communion matters little. The *spirit* is the all-important factor. The Samaritan woman was concerned about the place of worship, for, to the Jew, the temple signified the location of God's presence. Christ, however, gave utterance to a new revelation concerning prayer and worship.:"*God is Spirit, and they who worship him must worship him in spirit and in truth*" (John 4:24). Now, through grace, we can converse with God anywhere:

+ Jacob found that desert stones can become an altar. (See Genesis 32:22–30.)

+ Jonah prayed in the belly of a fish. (See Jonah 2:1.)

+ Hagar cried out to God in the heart of a desert. (See Genesis 21:16.)

+ Hezekiah prayed to the Lord on his sickbed. (See Isaiah 38:1–3.)

+ David, hiding in his cave, sought the Lord. (See Psalm 142.)

God's ear is open to our cry, whether by the riverside (see Acts 16:13), on the seashore (see Acts 21:5), on a housetop (see Acts 10:9), on a mountain (see Luke 6:12; 9:28), or on a battlefield (see 1 Samuel 7:9).

> They who seek the throne of grace,
> Find that throne in every place;
> If we live a life of prayer,
> God is present everywhere.[12]

While, of course, the environment should be as favorable as possible, when we come before God, it is blessed to know that we can pray inwardly, if not outwardly, in the most unfavorable surroundings. We can learn to shut the door, even amid conditions that would otherwise bring disturbance. Said the apostle Paul, *"I will therefore that men pray every where, lifting up holy hands"* (1 Timothy 2:8).

Ordinarily, prayer should have a place. *"When thou prayest, enter into thy closet, and when thou hast shut thy door, pray to thy Father"* (Matthew 6:6). Many saints have a place made sacred by habitual meetings with God. Bishop Handley Moule loved to pray and meditate as he walked in his garden. It is essential, if at all possible, to have a definite place, as secluded as possible, where we can be free from distraction and interruption, and where we can pray audibly, thereby guarding ourselves against wandering thoughts. Where there is a will to find "a place where Jesus sheds the oil of gladness on our heads,"[13] there will be a way to find such a place.

---

12. Oliver Holden, "They Who Seek the Throne of Grace," 1835.
13. Hugh Stowell, "From Every Stormy Wind," 1828.

THE POSTURE FOR PRAYER

No exclusive posture is prescribed in the Bible. It is certain that God would have us shun all slovenly habits when we assume a prayer attitude. "All the great non-Christian religions," Samuel Zwemer reminds us, "put emphasis on the right posture in their minute regulations of public and private prayer." The Bible associates several postures or gestures with prayer. We have, for example,

1. The lifting up of hands, a customary attitude adopted both in prayer and praise. (See Nehemiah 8:6; Psalm 28:2; 1 Timothy 2:8.) The lifting up of hands toward heaven became a synonym for prayer itself. (See Psalm 141:2.) Charles Wesley had this posture in mind when he wrote:

> Father, I stretch my hands to Thee,
> No other hope I know;
> If Thou withdraw Thyself from me,
> Ah! whither shall I go?[14]

2. Sitting is another rabbinical posture. In David's prayer of gratitude, we find him sitting. (See 1 Samuel 7:8.) Some writers affirm that this is the least reverent attitude of the body and should not be taken as a precedent. Possibly, because of his old age, David was obliged to sit. In such a matter, let every believer be fully persuaded in his own mind. Personally, the writer has his most blessed hours when "sitting before the Lord."

3. Standing was the usual Jewish attitude of prayer. (See 1 Samuel 1:26; Nehemiah 4; Mark 11:25.) Subjects usually stand in the presence of their sovereign. Hannah, praying for her son (see 1 Samuel 1:11–12); Solomon, blessing the congregation (see 1 Kings 8); Jeremiah, offering his intercession (see

---

14. Charles Wesley, "Father, I Stretch My Hands to Thee," 1741.

Jeremiah 29:7)—all stood. The Pharisees, the disciples, and the publican all stood as they prayed. Many, because of affliction, are not able to stand. In public prayer, it may be fitting to stand. Preachers, however, should not be overlong in praying, if the people are called upon to stand. Weary mothers and hardworking men have been on their feet long enough.

4. Kneeling is a reverent attitude adopted by others. Daniel (see Daniel 6:10), Stephen (see Acts 7:60), and Peter and Paul (see Ephesians 3:14) all knelt, at least at times. In biblical times, prayer was offered kneeling or standing, with prostration at the beginning and the end.

5. Prostration is another biblical posture. Ezekiel fell on his face—prostrated himself—as he beheld the glory of the Lord. (See Ezekiel 3:23; 9:8; 11:13). This was also the posture of Christ in Gethsemane. (See Luke 22:44.)

6. Eyes were usually open during prayer. The publican *"would not lift up so much as his eyes unto heaven"* (Luke 18:13). Jesus prayed with open eyes. (See Mark 6:41; 7:34; John 17:1.) How we came by the custom of closed eyes when praying is uncertain. Certainly closed eyes shut out so much around that would distract our attention.

While posture is of minor importance, yet careless habits cannot yield much power in prayer. We must choose those postures of the members of our body best fitted to our own realization of the divine presence, and not condemn others who adopt different habits, ever remembering that...

> 'Tis not to those who stand erect,
> Or those who bend the knee,
> It is to those who bend the heart
> The Lord will gracious be;
> It is the posture of the soul

That pleases, or offends;
If it be not in God's sight right,
Naught else can make amends.

THE PERIOD FOR PRAYER

The time we give to prayer is governed by desire, need, circumstances, and physical ability. Often, we hear the remark, "I have so little time for prayer." Because of its necessity, we must *make* time to converse with God. The most active life needs prayer the most. Well might the engine driver say that he has no time to take on coal and water, as the Christian to say he has no time for prayer. James Stalker, in his *Imago Christi*, reminds us that "Jesus appears to have devoted Himself specially to prayer at times when His life was unusually full of work and excitement…. Many in our day know what this congestion of occupation is: they are swept off their feet with their engagements and can scarcely find time to eat. We make this a reason for not praying; Jesus made it a reason for praying. Is there any doubt about which is the better course?"[15]

One cannot prescribe a hard-and-fast rule about periods of prayer for another. This is a matter of individual responsibility. The Bible enjoins us to pray at all seasons (see Ephesians 6:18) and to pray without ceasing (see 1 Thessalonians 5:17). The saints who have been mightily used of God have been those who made time for prayer a notable feature of their lives:

+ Charles Simeon devoted four hours a day to definite prayer.

+ Charles Wesley, the renowned hymnist, gave two hours daily to prayer.

+ John Wesley rose at four to pray, deeming this his greatest task.

---

15. Rev. James Stalker, D. D., *Imago Christi* (New York: Armstrong & Son, 1890), 139.

- Bishop Lancelot Andrews spent five hours daily in prayer and meditation. No wonder his *Private Devotions* is an immortal spiritual classic.

- John Fletcher sometimes prayed all night.

- Martin Luther had to spend three hours a day in prayer.

- Bishop Thomas Ken was with God before the clock struck three each morning.

- Joseph Alleine rose at four and felt ashamed if he heard tradesmen at work before him.

- John Welch, the mighty Scottish preacher, felt a day was lost if he did not spend eight to ten hours in prayer.

- Judson of Burma, the strong advocate of prayer, said that time must be given to God. Begin at midnight, then dawn, and during the day half a dozen times, was his advice.

Space fails us to speak of David Brainerd, David Livingstone, Hudson Taylor, Mary Slessor, Praying Hyde, and James Gilmore, as well as a host of others who cause us to hang our heads in shame when we say we have so little time for prayer.

The Bible makes it clear that we can pray at any time, for God never sleeps, and His ear is ever open to our cry. If, amid the cares, irksome duties, and responsibilities of life, we want to know the best time for the culture of the soul by prayer and meditation, Bible saints offer a variety of periods:

Daniel prayed upon his knees three times a day. (See Daniel 6:10.)

David was accustomed to pray evening, morning, and at noon. (See Psalm 55:17.) If he wrote a latter psalm, then seven times a day he praised the Lord. (See Psalm 119:164.)

Paul urged the saints to pray at all times and unceasingly. Paul and Silas prayed and praised at the midnight hour. (See Acts 16:25.)

Jesus prayed early in the morning, sometimes all night. He had to pray. It was His life. That is why often we read of Him alone in prayer and ever continuing in prayer. What a tense prayer life was the Master's! *"Being in an agony, he prayed"* (Luke 22:44). He arose *"a great while before day, he went out, and departed into a solitary place, and there prayed"* (Mark 1:35). No wonder He urged His own *"always to pray, and not to faint"* (Luke 18:1).

Summarizing Bible teaching as to the time element in prayer, we note:

REGULAR PRAYER

Busy men like David and Daniel were careful to let nothing interfere with their devotions. (See Psalm 55:17; Daniel 6:10.) Matthew Hale, late Lord Chief Justice of England, gave as this advice: "Be obstinately constant in your devotions at certain set times." Your circumstances will determine the best time for you.

MORNING PRAYER

No matter how brief a period we can give to morning prayer, the opening of the day is the best time, for then the mind is freshest, and we are freest from distraction. With one of old, we, too, should seek the face of God before we see the face of man.

Thy first transaction be
With God Himself above,
So shall thy business prosper well,
And all the day be love.[16]

EVENING PRAYER

When the day is over, we need to ask pardon for the sins of the day, to express our gratitude for God's mercies through the day, and then to seek His protection through the night. (See

16. Horatius Bonar, "Begin the Day with God," date unknown.

Psalm 4:8; 42:8; 141:2.) George Herbert wrote, "Who goes to bed and does not pray, maketh two nights of every day."

It may be that if we have had an exhausting day at home or business, we are too physically and mentally tired to spend much time in prayer. Many a weary worker has fallen asleep on his knees. Mary Slessor, the Scottish missionary who became known as "The White Queen of Calabar," was so worn out one day after mixing cement and building a new church that when she came to retire, she tumbled into bed praying, "Ye ken, Lord, I'm tired!"

Make no doubt about it, the pitying Master understood and accepted such a prayer; for it is not the length of a prayer, but the spirit of it that counts with Him. Robert Murray M'Cheyne once wrote, "I ought not to give up the good old habit of praying before going to bed; but guard must be kept against sleep. Planning what things I am to ask is the best remedy."

NOONDAY PRAYER

At noon, the two hands of the clock point in the same direction—upward. There is no need to pause and assume any prayer posture. No matter where we may be, knowing that the hands of the clock are heavenward at noon, we can pray within and bless God for His continual goodness. (See Acts 10:9.) We can sing:

> At noon, beneath the Rock
> Of ages, rest and pray;
> Sweet is that shadow from the heat,
> When the sun smites by day.[17]

WHISPERED PRAYER

Dr. Frank Laubach, in his most unusual book *Prayer, the Mightiest Force in the World*, wrote of "flash prayers, swift prayers, broadcast prayers, whisper prayers." Nehemiah was a conspicuous

17. James Montgomery, "Come to the Morning Prayer," 1854.

example of quick prayer. (See Nehemiah 2:4; 4:5; 5:19; 6:9, 14; 13:14, 22, 29, 31.) The apostles also made use of this type of prayer when immediate need arose. (See Matthew 8:25; 14:30; 15:25; John 4:49.) The quickest way to counteract the fiery darts of the enemy as they unexpectedly approach us is by the fervent darts of prayer. Let us guard, however, against pressing all our period of prayer into "flash" petitions.

We can learn to pray by the clock if we cannot pray by the heartbeat and thereby fix a prayer habit beneficial in its exercise. Dr. Laubach exhorted us to "use chunks of idle, wasted time to send up dart prayers. Upon awaking in the morning. In the bath. Dressing. Walking downstairs. Asking grace at table. Leaving the house. Riding or walking to work. Entering the elevator. Between interviews. Preparing for lunch. And a hundred more chunks all day long, until crawling into bed and falling asleep."

The best of us are conscious of the fact that we need God every moment of every minute, and all day long. Therefore, our entire life should become a prayer. Further, because of our constant need, we must take time to pray.

Edith H. Kenney's lines are apt at this point:

> There is always a time in the morning's prime,
> And the golden noontide fair;
> There is always time 'neath the evening chime,
> There is always time for prayer.
> When your weary feet falter in the path,
> Though to pause you do not dare,
> Would you find the stress of the day grow less?
> There is always time for prayer.

Can it be that these lines are being read by one who has for-saken the altar? Success, love, business, home, and the cares of life have crowded out prayer for your days. You used to take time to be holy and to speak often with your Lord. Now, you give Him only a passing word—if any at all. Have you become prayerless? If so, just put this book down, go to your knees, and ask God to restore unto you your lost passion for prayer.

THE PHASES OF PRAYER

Because our prayer life has its corporate and personal aspects, let us briefly consider one or two biblical modes for prayer.

UNITED PRAYER

It has been said that a man is only half of himself; his friends are the other half of him. How true this is in respect to prayer. There are times when a person can labor on his own; at other times, a team is needed. Many of us struggle with burdens that could have been lifted long ago, if only we had asked others to pray with and for us.

Think of the way the Word of God exalts the value of united prayer! (See Matthew 18:19–20; Daniel 2:17–18.) The limit of those gathering for united prayer is fixed downward at the lowest possible number, not enough to form a quorum—two or three. Numbers are not important, as long as those banded together for prayer are *"with one accord"* (Acts 1:14; 2:1, 46; 4:24.) It is from the Greek word for *"accord"* that we get our English word *symphony,* implying harmony of thought and feeling.

> The saints in prayer appear as one
> In word, in deed, and mind;
> While the Father and the Son
> Sweet fellowship they find.[18]

Unison in prayer greatly helps to banish the spirit of self-independence and narrowness of personal outlook, and it benefits

---

18. James Montgomery, "Prayer Is the Soul's Sincere Desire," 1818.

our spiritual life in general. That is why we should love the prayer meeting of the church—and we mean *prayer* meeting, such as that in which the church of Jesus Christ was born. (See Acts 1:4; 2:1, 42; 12:4; 16:13.) Such a meeting is ever the spiritual thermometer of a church. We have a striking example of the power of united prayer in Ezra 9–10.

Note:

a. Those assembled together (see Ezra 9:4)

b. How the number increased (see Ezra 10:1)

c. A shared burden and confession (see Ezra 10:2)

d. Renewal of consecration vows (see Ezra 10:3)

e. Cooperation because of prayer based upon concern (see Ezra 9:5)

f. Genuine humiliation, shame, and contrition (see Ezra 9:6–7)

g. Acknowledgment of God's grace and mercy (see Ezra 9:8)

h. Recognition of a door of opportunity (see Ezra 9:9)

What a forceful illustration Ezra gave us of united prayer resulting in revival! How the war-weary world needs similar praying groups! Unity in prayer means much to the cause of Christ among men. When in a prayer meeting, we should keep praying all through the meeting. We should cultivate a deep consciousness of God's presence and continue pleading, even when not praying audibly.

FAMILY PRAYER

Family prayer goes back to the early days of the Bible, when the head of the household was considered "the priest." Wherever the patriarchs pitched their tents, they erected an altar. (See, for example, Genesis 12:7–8; 13:3–4; 18:19.) We read of examples of the church in the local home. (See Romans 16:5; 1 Corinthians 16:19; Colossians 4:15; Philemon 2.) A home with an altar is a God-blessed home. Someone has said that "a home without prayer is like a house without a roof." Is yours a roofless house? The hope of America is not in its military might or economic devices but in its altars. A family altar in each of the country's millions of homes would make America the mightiest spiritual force the world has ever known.

What about your home? Is it professedly religious, yet destitute of an altar? Did you have one, and has it been broken down? Erect it again. Get back to your Bethel, and many of your family troubles will cease. An anonymous writer of the year 1600 penned these memorable lines:

> Whom God hath made the heads of families
> He hath made priests to offer sacrifice;
> Daily let part of Holy Writ be read,
> Let, as the body, so the soul have bread:
> For look how many souls in thy house be
> With just as many souls God trusteth thee.

SECRET PRAYER

While Scripture records instances of public, united prayer, it also has much to say about secret prayer. In Matthew 6:6, our Lord spoke of the place of prayer, saying, *"Enter into thy closet."* Then, He drew attention to the privacy of prayer: *"Shut thy door."* Alas, it is sadly possible to shut our closet door on the world as a sphere, and yet to carry the atmosphere of the world into that closet!

The world will never know—neither will we as individuals— how the secret prayers of others on our behalf have influenced our lives. Dr. J. H. Jowett had his closet. It was an upper room in his home in which were two chairs—one always vacant—a table, and nothing else, save for a Bible. Seated in one chair, Dr. Jowett would converse with his Lord, whom he imagined to be in the other chair. Here, he spent hours with his Master, poring over the Word.

Jesus taught us to *"pray to thy Father which is in secret"* (Matthew 6:6), for when we are alone with God, we can unbosom ourselves. What cannot be told to human ears can be poured into His sympathetic ear. Alone with Him, we can speak intimately about our unsaved loved ones. We can converse with Him about each one of them with the assurance that He who hears will answer. Praying thusly, we come to know what it is to be rewarded openly. No one knows of our prayers, but we see them changing both people and circumstances. Of course, we ourselves are changed, for secret prayer transforms those who pray thusly. (See 2 Corinthians 3:18; Exodus 34:29–30.)

Is it not true that the saints of all ages have been men of the prayer closet? They proved that "solitude is the mother country of the strong." Recall some of these spiritual giants:

- Abraham, when great darkness covered him, kept lonely vigil over his sacrifice.

- Moses, at the burning bush in the desert, was alone with God.

- Elijah, on Mt. Carmel and in the cave, also experienced the blessedness of aloneness with God.

- David Livingstone, on his knees in his Chitambo hut, prayed and died alone.

- British Major-General C. G. Gordon, entering his tent, left a white handkerchief outside to denote he was alone in prayer and was not to be disturbed.

- The secret place of Jonathan Edwards was on the banks of the Hudson River.

- David Brainerd spoke of his "secret prayer...in the woods."

+ Richard W. Oliver, a flaming herald who died so young, spoke of his trysting place by "an old oak tree."

+ Robert Murray M'Cheyne had his secret place. Years later, an old sexton of St. Peter's, Dundee, would take visitors to M'Cheyne's study and say, "That's the chair he used to sit in for hours with his head in his hands, shedding tears."

Jesus had His sacred garden spot, to which He often resorted to pray. Judas knew the place, and perhaps the most despicable aspect of his crime was that he led Christ's enemies to that hideaway of secret prayer.

Commenting upon the book of James, George Williams gave us this helpful summary of the phases of prayer in his *Student's Commentary*:

1. Personal Prayer: *"Let **him** pray"* (James 5:13, emphasis added).

2. United Prayer: *"Let **them** pray"* (James 5:14, emphasis added).

3. Believing Prayer: *"The prayer of **faith**"* (James 5:15, emphasis added).

4. Mutual Prayer: *"Pray for **one another**"* (James 5:16, emphasis added).

5. Operative Prayer: *"**Effectual**, fervent prayer"* (James 5:16, emphasis added).

6. Earnest Prayer: *"He prayed **earnestly**"* (James 5:17, emphasis added).

7. Continued Prayer: *"He prayed **again**"* (James 5:18, emphasis added).

Wonderful indeed are the habits and habitat of prayer. Method is of no great consequence—whether we pray in silence, like Hannah; in secret thought, like Nehemiah; aloud, like the Syrophoenician woman; in tears, like Mary Magdalene; or in joy, like Paul.

Age likewise does not count. Children, like Samuel; youth, like Daniel and his friends; fully grown adults, like the centurion; or the elderly, like old Simeon, can all speak to God.

Position and nationality form no barrier to prayer. Whether black or white, red or yellow, male or female, rich or poor, saved or lost—all can come to God in His appointed way. The one thing to remember is that we cannot pray by proxy. No priest can act on our behalf in prayer. Prayer must be a personal, living force in the individual life.

CHAPTER 8

THE PATTERN OF PRAYER

Perfect prayer patterns are scattered throughout the Bible. Observance of their underlying principles and organization is of immense help when we come to frame our own petitions. When Jesus said to His disciples, *"After this manner therefore pray ye"* (Matthew 6:9), He never implied that they were to take His words and use them as stereotyped literature. He was setting out a plan of approach. He referred to the spirit and general features of prayer, as we shall presently see. While much of the rich and expressive prayer phraseology of Bible saints will unconsciously become part of our prayers—and the strongest prayers are those saturated with Scripture—we must be careful not merely to reiterate the prayer language of others. Seeking the Spirit's aid in our intercessions, we must cultivate a clear accent of our own. Remember that David could not fight in Saul's armor—the sling and the pebble were more natural to the shepherd lad.

The wealth of material at our disposal in respect to prayer examples is great and varied, but we can indicate only a few guides.

ABRAHAM

The *"friend of God"* (James 2:23) stands out as a spiritual giant in the realm of prayer. His prayer of intercession for the city of Sodom is incomparable. (See Genesis 18:23–33.) In another record of Abraham's communion with God, we have a pattern of the listening prayer. (See Genesis 13:14–18.) Too often, prayer becomes a one-sided exercise where we do all the talking. Here, God spoke to His friend. Note four aspects of this neglected side of prayer:

1. It was the place of separation. *"The* LORD *said unto Abram, after that Lot was separated from him"* (Genesis 13:14). Certain company hinders fellowship with God.

2. It was the place of vision. *"Lift up now thine eyes, and look from the place where thou art northward, and southward, and eastward, and westward"* (Genesis 13:14). If too absorbed with the daily round and the common task, we become blind to eternal realities.

3. It was the place of promise. *"All the land which thou seest, to thee will I give it, and to thy seed for ever"* (Genesis 13:15). Prayer gives us the authority to claim divine promises.

4. It was the place of power. *"Arise, walk through the land in the length of it and in the breadth of it; for I will give it unto thee"* (Genesis 13:17). In prayer, we not only receive God's call, but also His power to obey and follow Him fully.

JACOB

In his prayer with the wrestling angel, Jacob was on holy ground. His experience guides our hearts and minds as we come to take hold of God. In the agony of prayer, his own strength failed him. At the end of his own resources, he received the blessing of his Divine Wrestler. (See Genesis 32:26–29.)

MOSES

Moses offered one of the boldest prayers in the Bible. (See Numbers 14:17–24.) Utterly self-forgetful, Moses pleaded the covenant promises of God. The divine response to such intercessory prayer was immediate and embracive. Other intercessions of Moses guide the way in prayer. Let's examine Exodus 5:15–6:9. Note how he faced the trials of leadership:

1. Amid crisis and criticism, Moses turned to God, and his prayer was twofold. Nothing but trouble had come his way since he had approached Pharaoh; the promised deliverance had not taken place. (See Exodus 5:22–23.)

2. Moses gained an insight into the infinite patience of God. "*Then the* Lord *said…*" (Exodus 6:1). Human impatience was met with divine patience.

3. Moses received a great and satisfying answer. "*Now shalt thou see…*" (Exodus 6:1). Amid the disheartenments and disappointments of his leadership, Moses learned that God was with him, if only he would follow God and be ready to do His will.

HANNAH

Hannah provides us with a woman's prayer of thanksgiving and triumph. (See 1 Samuel 1:26–2:3.) What a great soul Hannah was! Her story is one of rare delicacy. Arising out of faith and hope, her prayer for a son was answered. She knew the secret and power of prayer. Follow these three aspects of Hannah's prayer:

1. She offered God a noble prayer of thanksgiving.

2. In her prayer song, there was a solemn dedication.

3. Hannah expressed a heart-inspiring confession of faith.

HEZEKIAH

Here is another whose prayer is worthy of emulation. (See Isaiah 37.) Mark these stages of Hezekiah's prayer in the first verse:

1. *"He rent his clothes,"* revealing deep concern.
2. *"He put on sackcloth,"* showing true humiliation.
3. *"He went into the house of the* LORD," there to worship.

Then, Hezekiah made confession (see verse 3), expressed his hope (see verse 4), spread his trouble before the Lord (see verse 14), and made his petition (see verse 15).

OTHER EXAMPLES

Other prominent examples of prayer are those of Isaac (see Genesis 25:21), Job (see the book of Job), Melchizedek (see Genesis 14:19–20), Lot (see Genesis 19:19), Salaam (see Numbers 22), Manasseh (see 2 Chronicles 33:12), and Isaiah (see Isaiah 64), all alike so full of faith in God.

Let us conclude with a word about David, who gave us no theoretical lessons about prayer. No one in the Old Testament can teach us so much about our approach to God as David. How rich and varied his prayers were! David led us right into "the prayer laboratory." Here is one of his matchless prayers, so apropos for a time like this, when the world is so topsy-turvy.

> LORD, *how are they increased that trouble me! Many are they that rise up against me. Many there be which say of my soul, there is no help for him in God. But thou, O* LORD, *art a shield for me; my glory, and the lifter up of mine head. I cried unto the* LORD *with my voice, and he heard me out of his holy hill. I laid me down and slept; I awaked; for the* LORD *sustained me. I will not be afraid of ten thousands of people, that have set themselves against me round about. Arise, O* LORD; *save me, O my God: for thou hast smitten all mine enemies upon the cheek bone; thou hast broken the teeth of the ungodly.*

Salvation belongeth unto the LORD: thy blessing is upon thy
people.   *(Psalm 3:1–8)*

Examining this priceless example, we have six phases:

1. A complaint to God about the diversity of foes and David's discouragement. (See verses 1–2.)

2. David's consciousness of being God-encircled. (See verse 3.)

3. A cry to God, resulting in rest and refreshment. (See verses 4–5.)

4. A confidence in God that prayer changes things. (See verse 6.)

5. A call on God, because courage, while prayerless, is foolish. (See verse 7.)

6. A confession that God is the source of all salvation. (See verse 8.)

The New Testament abounds in types and examples of prayer. What a gallery of prayer warriors blazing the way to a more exalted prayer life it presents! With its richer and fuller revelation of divine truth, the New Testament brings us clearer light regarding the duty and privilege of prayer.

In the Old Testament, God had a temple for His people; in the New Testament, He has a people *as* His temple. Under the gospel, the saints have superior advantages in their intercourse and communion with God. As we have related, Old Testament prayers were, for the most part, associated with temporal blessings. In the New Testament, we are urged to pray for, and seek after, spiritual blessings. (See Ephesians 1:3.)

Grace places believers on vantage ground much higher than God's people enjoyed prior to the fuller revelation of Christ and His apostles. Specific instructions are given for the guidance of those seeking spiritual gifts and graces. Promises and assurances are cited for the purpose of inspiring the most timid with confidence. A further advantage a Christian has over the Old Testament saint is that of presenting his petitions in the name of Jesus Christ.

Ask in my name.... (John 14:13; 16:26)

Hitherto [mark this word] *have ye asked nothing in my name.* (John 16:24)

Ancient believers could pray, and they did, but not in the peerless name of Jesus, even though they were accepted through the future propitiatory sacrifice of Christ. *"Abraham rejoiced to see my day"* (John 8:56), said Christ.

Furthermore, church saints have the added advantage of Christ's intercession on their behalf. He pledged Himself to act on behalf of His own as their *personal* intercessor. *"I will pray the Father for you"* (John 16:26). This was a completely new revelation—an announcement and an assurance that no Old Testament believer ever had.

> Great Advocate! almighty Friend!
> On Him our humble hopes depend;
> Our cause can never, never fail,
> For Jesus pleads, and must prevail.[19]

As a higher encouragement to His saints, Christ assured them that He will Himself answer their supplications. *"Whatsoever ye shall ask in my name, that will I do.... If ye shall ask any thing in my name, I will do it"* (John 14:13–14).

Another advantage in the matter of prayer brought by the New Testament is the ministry of the Holy Spirit. The Jews of old knew very little about the third Person of the Trinity. It was the death, resurrection, and ascension of Christ that liberated the gift of the

19. Anne Steele, "He Lives, the Great Redeemer Lives," 1760.

Spirit on our behalf. One purpose of His ministry is to awaken and maintain a spirit of prayer within believers. The indispensable importance of such a gift is that believers have a guarantee that their prayers are heard and answered as they pray in and by the Spirit.

Approaching, then, the privileges of New Testament believers, what else can we do but exclaim with the hymnist, "'Tis a broad land, of wealth unknown"? Would that with all our advantages over a darker dispensation, we had the same power with God as saints like Moses, Elijah, and Daniel. How they could storm heaven with amazing results! What holy intimacy seemed to exist between God and those men! With all our added privileges, our prayer life should be more vital and dynamic than it was in Old Testament days. But is it?

Since the previous chapters of this book are filled with examples and exhortations concerning prayer taken from the lives and teachings of Christ and His apostles, it is not deemed necessary to dwell on instances of prayer in the New Testament, as we did when dealing with the Old Testament.

THE PRAYERS OF CHRIST

Preachers may find this bare outline serviceable. It contains examples of Jesus' prayers...

1. Over the healing of the lepers (see Matthew 8:1–4)

2. When the storm arose (see Matthew 8:23–27)

3. In connection with healings (see Matthew 9:18–31; Mark 1:35; Luke 4:42)

4. Concerning the revelation of God (see Matthew 11:25–27)

5. At the grave of Lazarus (see John 11:38–44)

6. For the security and sanctification of His own (see John 17)

7. In dark Gethsemane (see Matthew 26:39, 42–44)

8. Related to His death (see Matthew 27:46; Luke 23:41–44; John 12:27–33)

It may be found profitable to observe one or two characteristic features of our Lord's prayer ministry:

1. He loved a solitary place for prayer. (See Matthew 14:23; Mark 1:35; 6:46; John 6:15.) Christ believed in the morning watch. Do we?

2. He believed in praying for His enemies. (See Matthew 5:44; Luke 6:28.) At the cross, He prayed for His murderers— Romans and Jews. The Romans were the immediate agents of His death; the Jews were the instigators of it.

3. He abhorred mere show in prayer. (See Matthew 6:5, 8.) It is not the length of our prayers but their quality that counts. Christ's own supplications were remarkably short.

4. He believed in method in prayer. (See Matthew 6:9.) The Lord's Prayer is the model, unequaled in its beauty and comprehensiveness. As Alexander Pope said, "Order is heaven's first law."

5. He sought for wisdom and guidance in solitude. (See Luke 6:12.) Faced with the choice of disciples, Christ retired from the interruption of the world. "Cold mountains and the midnight air, witness'd the fervor of His prayer."[20] Have we learned that devotional solitude "is commended by high example, and commanded by the high authority of the Savior"[21]?

6. He advocated fervent, importunate prayer and its propriety. (See Luke 18:1–8; James 5:16.) Perseverance in prayer is advocated in three key words: *ask, seek, knock.*

20. Isaac Watts, "My Dear Redeemer and My Lord," 1707.
21. Robert Philip, *Devotional Guides*, Volume 1 (New York: Robert Carter, 1848), 214.

Then earnest let us be,
And never faint in prayer;
God loves our importunity,
And makes our cause His care.[22]

7. He taught that true humility should accompany prayer. (See Luke 18:9–13.) Intercourse with God must be accompanied by lowliness of heart. If prayer is to be acceptable, it must rise from an altar on which humility has been the first sacrifice. If we would be accepted of God, as we pray, we must shun the vain glory and offensive ostentation of the Pharisees. Christ stoutly condemned it in the parable before us.

8. He sought the will of God on His knees. (See Luke 22:39–44.) The ruling passion of Christ's life was to know His Father's will and to get it done. Note that He had to pray three times before the full revelation came.

9. His prayers were saturated with tears. (See Hebrews 5:7.) Perhaps ours are ineffectual because they are too dry.

10. He continues His prayer ministry in heaven. (See Hebrews 4:14–16.)

Other prayers worthy of notice in the Gospels are those of Zacharias (see Luke 1:10–18), the Syrophoenician woman (see Matthew 15:22–29), Bartimaeus (see Mark 10:46–52), the apostles (see Luke 17:5–6), the thief (see Luke 23:39–43), the Samaritan woman (see John 4:9–15), and the nobleman (see John 4:46–50).

The book of Acts, which some refer to as the "fifth gospel" of the New Testament, is saturated with prayer. The early church was so dynamic in its witness. Why? It lived on its knees. The church was born in prayer and, living in such an atmosphere, turned the world upside-down. (See Acts 1:14.) Whenever the saints prayed,

22. Origin unknown.

something happened. Trace these prayers and use them as a series for prayer-meeting meditations: Acts 1:14, 24; 2:42; 3:1; 4:23–31; 6:4–7, 10; 7:59; 8:4, 15; 9:4–6, 11, 40; 10:2, 9; 12:5, 12; 14:23; 16:13, 16, 25; 21:5; 27:35. In fact, an acrostic for Acts forms a list of the types of prayer found in the book: Adoration, Confession, Thanksgiving, Supplication.

THE PRAYERS OF PAUL

Paul was preeminently a man of prayer. As soon as he was saved, he was found praying. He was strong in prayer. He could turn a prison cell into a prayer chamber. (See Acts 16:25.)

Charles Spurgeon once said, "Prayer is a creature's strength, his very breath and being." A study of Paul's life and labors proves that prayer was his "breath and being," perhaps more than it was for any other man. The apostle's prayers afford masterpieces of intercession unexcelled in the devotional literature of any age or country.

A remarkable feature of Paul's prayers is that they were conceived on the highest plane of spiritual living. They breathe the air of heaven and serve to lift our prayer life to a higher level. Would that we had space to offer a full exposition of Paul's matchless prayers, as well as of what he taught concerning prayer:

1. Prayer for divine power (see Ephesians 1:15–20)

2. Prayer for knowledge and power (see Ephesians 1:15–21)

3. Prayer for a personal Pentecost (see Ephesians 3:13–21)

4. Prayer for perseverance in godliness (see Philippians 1:9–11)

5. Prayer for spiritual perception (see Colossians 1:9–13).

6. Prayer for perfection of faith and love (see 1 Thessalonians 3:9–13)

7. Prayer for complete sanctification
   (see 1 Thessalonians 5:23–24)

8. Prayer for the fulfillment of God's will
   (see 2 Thessalonians 1:11–12)

9. Prayer for deliverance from evil men (see 2 Thessalonians 3:1–5)

10. Prayer for tranquility of heart (see 2 Thessalonians 3:16)

11. Prayer for stability in life and service (see 2 Thessalonians 3:16)

12. Prayer for a well-pleasing life (see Hebrews 13:20–21)

The last book of the Bible, Revelation, records the prayers of the godly and the godless. Study the book from this angle. Do verses such as Revelation 5:8 and 8:3 imply that no Spirit-inspired prayer will go unanswered? Are our presently unanswered prayers treasured up by God to be answered in His own way and time? Wonderful, is it not, that the Bible closes with a prayer for the coming of Him who is our mighty, heavenly Intercessor? (See Revelation 22:20.)

Saints at prayer in the days of the apostles teach us what a Christian poet has beautifully expressed:

> In every joy that crowns my days,
> In every pain I bear,
> My heart shall find delight in praise,
> Or seek relief in prayer.[23]

Throughout the New Testament, prayer is proved to be a mighty force. "The prayer of faith moves the hand of Him that moveth all things." May grace be ours to appropriate, as the apostles could, the power that prayer can liberate in and through our lives!

Another truth our hearts dare not miss is that if we would be heard and answered as we pray, we must live in consistence with

---

23. H. M. Williams, "Habitual Devotion," c. 1866.

our daily supplications. Nothing about our person and performance must contradict our prayer.

Studying the prayer examples of the Bible, we arrive at the conclusion that one of the greatest assets of prayer is its character-training power. The life of the person of prayer, and those prayed for, undergoes a change. Take, for instance, the prayers of Paul. Consistently, he kept Christian character in view. Read Ephesians 1:16–23; 3:14–21; Philippians 1:9–11; Colossians 1:9–12; and 1 Thessalonians 3:11–13, and see what kind of men and women such prayers would produce. Prayer is valueless if it is not character-forming.

The pattern prayers that we have set forth would further seem to indicate that there are four governing principles and prepositions to observe:

1. *For:*. Asking is to be specific. (See Matthew 7:7–8.)

2. *With:* The Spirit is our prayer-helper. (See Romans 8:26.)

3. *Against:* Satan and sin are foes of prayer. (See Ephesians 6:12.)

4. *Through:* Persistence must be practiced. (See Ephesians 6:18.)

CHAPTER 9

THE SCOPE OF PRAYER

While God's ear is universal, it is also endlessly discriminating. Some petitions, because of their nature, or because of the life of the petitioner, are never answered. Prayer as an exercise, however, covers all persons, places, and particulars. Prayer is a shortcut to the heart of God; therefore, we should be as universal as possible in our prayers. We can pray *"with all prayer...with all perseverance and supplication for all saints"* (Ephesians 6:18, emphasis added). It is always safe to intercede for others; none is too poor to offer such a gift, and none is too wealthy that he or she can give a richer one. Consider the wide range of prayer. We can...

+ pray for all men. (See 1 Timothy 2:1.)
+ pray about all things. (See John 15:16; Romans 8:32.)
+ pray for all saints. (See John 17:21; Ephesians 6:18.)
+ pray for Israel. (See Romans 10:1.)
+ pray for Gentiles. (See Luke 10:2.)
+ pray for rulers. (See 1 Timothy 2:2.)
+ pray for ministers. (See Ephesians 6:19.)
+ pray for conversions. (See 1 Timothy 2:1, 4.)
+ pray for personal enemies. (See Luke 6:28.)
+ pray for pardon after discovered sin. (See 1 John 1:9.)
+ pray for the sick. (See James 5:16.)
+ pray that the Spirit will show us how to pray. (See Romans 8:26.)

Let us endeavor to discover how prayer, in its scope, covers the personal, social, material, natural, spiritual, ecclesiastical, and national realms. *"Be careful for nothing; but in every thing by prayer and supplication with thanksgiving let your requests be made known unto God"* (Philippians 4:6). Here, the words *"nothing"* and *"every thing"* are all-embracing and all-inclusive in their scope. (See also Matthew 21:22; John 14:14.) Beyond these realms we cannot go. Prayers are related to all that we can see in the world around us. They do not have an eternal scope. The Bible grants no authority for prayers for the dead. Once a soul passes over into the "great beyond," he or she is outside the range of our prayers. Once physically dead, character is fixed, and no prayers of earth can influence such a person. Therefore, any religious system advocating prayers of the living for deceased relatives is guilty of cruel, heathen delusion.

As we seek to outline the theme on hand, we may wonder how God can possibly listen to countless millions all over the world, who, in their own language, present their own needs, cares, sorrows, and problems. A distinguishing characteristic of the greatest human minds is the ability to combine vast conceptions with attention to minute details. Thus is it with God. He can fashion stars and bind up broken hearts. (See Psalm 147:3, 4.) He combines majesty and lowliness. (See Isaiah 40:12, 15, 25; Luke 12:6–7.)

> Nothing to Him is little,
> Who is Himself so great;
> His hand is large for every need,
> His heart for every state.

Taking advantage of the promise *"whatsoever ye shall ask"* (Matthew 21:22; John 14:13; 15:16), we must, of course, leave the answer to Him. Our prayers are responded to not as we think, but as He knows best. He never fails to give the very best to those who leave the choice with Him. The Lord's choice is always *choice*. Then, let us do as the hymn says and, "in the presence of our Lord, unbosom all our cares"[24] and act on the advice of Hartley Coleridge: "If for any wish thou darest not pray, then pray for grace to cast that wish away."

THE PERSONAL REALM

Afflicted as we are with so many personal cares and needs, the bulk of our prayers are related to ourselves. The old Negro spiritual has it, "I'm standin' in the need o' prayer, O Lord." Wonderful, is it not, that we can retire into our closet and talk with the Lord about all that concerns our individual life? "*He shall call upon me, and I will answer him*" (Psalm 91:15).

Is trouble ours? Then let us hold on to God's promises, such as Psalm 50:15 and Psalm 86:7.

Is there a personal financial problem? We can claim divine relief from Psalm 69:33, Psalm 102:17, and Philippians 4:19.

Can it be that we face some phase of peril requiring protection? Let us plead Psalm 32:6–7 and Psalm 91:1–7.

Are we in doubt, needing guidance and direction in a choice that must be made? We should claim Isaiah 30:19–21 and Jeremiah 33:3.

Is there a conscience disturbed because of personal sin? Blessed to know we can tell it all to Him, who offers to pardon and deliver in Isaiah 55:6 and Romans 10:13.

Charlotte Elliott well expressed the benefits of prayer in these lines:

> Lord, till we reach yon blissful shore,
> No privilege so dear shall be,

---

24. John Newton, "Dear Shepherd of Thy People, Hear," 1779.

As thus my inmost souls to pour
In prayer to Thee![25]

A baby cries to attract attention, to get what he or she wants. Personal prayer must not be used thusly. The prodigal son prayed *"give me"* (Luke 15:12) and *"make me"* (Luke 15:19). Both requests were graciously answered. We should be grateful that God does not always answer our personal, unworthy prayers. "Self" is an intruder, even in the secret place. Alas, our prayers are too often motivated by a desire to realize our own wishes! In His mercy, God sometimes answers our prayers, although they may not be on a very high level. (See Judges 16:28.) He listens, although we do not know what we are asking for. (See Mark 10:35–45.)

When we center prayer on our petty, individual problems, using God for our own ends, as it were, prayer is futile. Prayers for ourselves must have as their end an increase in the value of the life we would give others. Jesus could pray, *"For their sakes I sanctify myself"* (John 17:19). Cloistered prayer should lead to world service.

THE SOCIAL REALM

Many of our prayers are answered through others; therefore, we must pray *for* others. A personal prayer life is always enriched when others are prayed for. Paul taught this truth. (See Romans 1:9; Philippians 1:4; Ephesians 1:15–16.) So did Christ exemplify it. (See Matthew 19:13; Mark 7:34; Luke 10:2; John 17:20.) We must not only pray with others but also pray for others. Selfish prayer shuts others out because it shuts God out. Unselfish prayers are ever rich in intercession, adoration, and grace. How blessed we are when we make mention of others in our prayers. (See Philemon 4.) Said William Wallace Horner in *Let Us Pray*, "The less we pray

25. Charlotte Elliott, "My God, Is Any Hour So Sweet," 1836.

for ourselves, and the more we pray for others, the nearer we will approach the spiritual conception of true prayer, and the greater assurance we will have that our prayers will be answered."

Prayer for others is the noblest type of prayer. Dr. Clarence Macartney reminds us that "the first prayer recorded in the Bible, the prayer of Abraham, was a prayer for others, his intercession for the cities of the plain. The last words of Christ to His disciples before His crucifixion were a prayer that they might be kept in the truth and from the evil that is in the world. Paul, when he knelt on the sands of Miletus, having finished all his ministry for the church at Ephesus, poured out his soul in intercession for the elders of that church."

In his chapter "Praying for Others," Dr. Macartney wrote of how such praying has a twofold benefit. First, prayer for others lifts the man who prays out of himself and brings to view the glories of life. Second, prayer for others benefits those for whom we pray.

The most conspicuous saints of the Bible practiced intercessory prayer. We have Job (see Job 42:7–10), Moses (see Exodus 8:12, 30; 9:33), Samuel (see 1 Samuel 7:7–9; 15:11), Elijah (see James 5:17–18), Ezra (see Ezra 9:5–15), Nehemiah (see Nehemiah 1:4–11), Jeremiah (see Jeremiah 7:16; 14:11), Paul (see Romans 1:9; Philippians 1:3–11), Stephen (see Acts 7:60), and Epaphras (see Colossians 4:12). Our blessed Lord continues this type of praying in heaven. (See Hebrews 7:25.)

Intercessory prayer brings us into *"the royal priesthood"* (1 Peter 2:9). How privileged we are to be associated with such divine peerage! This is a ministry that many can exercise who have been debarred from other aspects of Christian service, including invalids, the sick, and the elderly. Eternity alone will reveal what has been accomplished through the prayers of God's shut-in saints.

One of the marvelous features of social praying is that it reaches persons and places that could not be covered in any other way. It is the shortest route to reach the uttermost parts of the earth. How apt are the words of Tennyson:

> For so the whole round earth is every way
> Bound by gold chains about the feet of God.

Many of us owe more than we understand to those who are bound to us by human ties. Their prayers surround our life and service, and they greatly influence both. Archbishop Trench wrote beautifully of this aspect of our prayer ministry in a poem:

> When hearts are full of yearning tenderness
> For the loved absent, whom we cannot reach,
> By deed or token, gesture or kind speech,
> The spirit's true affection to express;
> Then like a cup capacious to contain
> The overflowing of the heart, is prayer.

We are apt to forget that prayers for our enemies are also definitely enjoined in Scripture, both by precept and example. (See Matthew 5:44; Luke 23:34; Acts 7:60; 2 Timothy 4:16.)

One day, Dr. Joseph Parker of the renowned City Temple, London, was preaching in Hyde Park when an infidel tried to shout him down with a question: "What did Christ do for Stephen when he was stoned?" Parker answered immediately, "He gave him grace to pray for those who stoned him." What a victory that was! Many believe that the dying prayers of Stephen for his murderers resulted in the conversion of Saul of Tarsus, who became the apostle Paul.

There are three principles to guide those who engage in intercessory prayer:

1. They must have a sincere desire for the highest interests of those for whom they pray.
2. They must have the utmost faith in God's promises and His sufficiency to meet the needs of those prayed for.
3. They must hold themselves in readiness to cooperate in action as an outcome of their prayers.

Such prayers take feet and go to those who are interceded for.

> Make me an intercessor,
> One who can really pray;
> One of the Lord's Remembrances
> By night as well as day!

THE MATERIAL REALM

Made of the dust, we need much that comes from the dust to maintain us: food, money, raiment, and other material necessities. Can we pray about these? Well, Jesus taught His own to pray, "*Give us this day our daily bread*" (Matthew 6:11). When George Müller needed bread and milk for his orphans, he never told anyone of his need. It was his principle that God alone should be informed. He was already cognizant of what the orphans required, and Müller believed that all he had to do was ask—and receive. Was not our Lord thinking of food and raiment when He spoke of the sparrows and the lilies? Yes, He is able to supply *all* our need, even our creaturely wants. He miraculously fed the Israelites for forty years. He saw that His hungry prophet Elijah was supplied with food, even though it meant commissioning a raven to bring it.

THE NATURAL REALM

Prayer is not merely a devotional exercise; it is also a dynamic force that brings one into contact with God, the Creator, the all-beneficent One. Martin Tupper spoke of prayer as "the tender nerve that moves the muscles of omnipotence."

While this type of prayer does not change God's plans, it does provide the means for carrying them into effect. It removes the obstacles from our part, enabling God to perform His will. Prayer links human impotence with divine omnipotence and brings the infinite resources of the infinite God into beneficial action. Prayer becomes, as Tennyson put it, "a breath that fleets beyond this iron world, and touches Him that made it."

Whether we think of the miracles God performed for the Israelites—the subduing of kingdoms and turning of enemies to flight; the closing of the mouths of lions; the quenching of fire;, the experiences of Elijah, Gideon, and Samson; the sun standing still; Jonah and the whale; the miracles of Jesus—the story is the same: God is able to accomplish great and mighty things on behalf of His own. Since He is the Creator, all laws are subject to His bidding. To refer to George Müller again, God caused the fog to lift for His servant, so that he could make his American speaking engagement in time.

> There's a power that man can wield
> When mortal aid is vain,
> That eye, that arm, that love to reach,
> That listening ear to gain.
> That power is prayer, which soars so high,
> Through Jesus to the throne,
> And moves the hand which moves the world
> To bring salvation down. [26]

THE SPIRITUAL REALM

Prayers related to sins and struggles in the spiritual realm abound in the Bible: Jacob at the brook (see Genesis 32), Job and

---

26. James Cowden Wallace, "There Is an Eye That Never Sleeps," 1895.

his mystery (see Job 14), David and his dark sin (see Psalm 51:39), and many others. When a person is conscious of sin, "confession is a fundamental element of prayer," says Ella Robertson. "There are times, too, when confession to some fellow man is what is needed to clear up our spiritual condition." Confession may have to be personal (see 2 Samuel 12; Psalm 51; 1 John 1:7–9) or national, as under the ministries of Ezra and Nehemiah. (See Ezra 9, Nehemiah 9.) That peace follows confession to God and others is amply proved in Psalm 32.

Under this section, we can briefly discuss prayer and temptation. (See Matthew 26:41.) We are not to pray that temptation may be kept from us but that we may be preserved from the evil lurking in the heart of any temptation. Temptation is a universal experience. All are tempted. Temptations may differ according to our heredity, environment, and age, but they come to all. Clarence Macartney said,

> There are temptations of the body, temptations of the mind, temptations of the spirit. Temptation is a great equalizer. It smites in youth; it smites in middle life; even the aged are not exempt from its cruel and dangerous sorrows, for...
>
> The gray-haired saint may fall at last,
>
> The surest guide a wanderer prove;
>
> Death only binds us fast
>
> To that bright shore of love.
>
> Temptation is a sleepless, unwearying enemy.... Great is the power of temptation, and great is the destructive power of a single temptation.... A single temptation not fought against with the divinely appointed weapon can ruin a character that has been slowly and painfully built through long years.

It is because of the fact, power, and danger of temptation that Jesus urged us to watch and pray. Watching and praying are practically equivalent, for when we are watching against temptation, we are praying against it; and when we are praying against it, we are on guard against it. When we pray, we bring ourselves into vital contact with Christ, who knows all about the wiles and stratagems of the devil. He met the enemy and triumphed gloriously over him, and He is therefore able to make us more than conquerors.

A British pilot had not flown very far before he noticed a peculiar noise. Looking down, he saw a rat gnawing away at a vital part of his plane. He could not stop to kill the rodent. What could he do? Up into the rarified air he zoomed, and the rat rolled over, dead. Does this not illustrate the power of prayer? When the rat of hell tempts us, prayer takes us up into the rare air of heaven, where everything not of God quickly dies.

THE ECCLESIASTICAL REALM

Everything related to church life comes within the scope of prayer. So many New Testament prayers are taken up with the concerns and character of the church of Jesus Christ. Paul's prayers for the churches he founded were rich in example and suggestion. The carnal Corinthians, the legalized Galatians, the confused Colossians, the troubled Thessalonians—all alike were surrounded with the apostle's mighty intercessions. The care of all the churches was his, but he knew how to cast such a burden upon the Lord. He prayed for all the churches to abound in love, to stand fast, to grow in grace, and to pray without ceasing. Paul never sinned in ceasing to pray for those whom God had helped him to win.

God would have us pray for the deepening of the church's spiritual life. Revival belongs to her. (See Psalm 85:6.) Revival brings the church into fuller fellowship with the Lord, who desires to use her in a world of need. The salvation of souls is the direct outcome of such a revival.

Samuel Zwemer, in a striking chapter dealing with prayer and missions, proved conclusively that the evangelization of the lost, at home and abroad, depended upon a revival of prayer within the church: "Since the beginning of the missionary enterprise, in the upper room at Jerusalem, prayer has been the secret of power and perseverance and victory. The history of missions is the history of answered prayer."

We have the entreaty of Jesus to pray to the Lord of the harvest to gather the multitudes in darkness, both here and in the regions beyond.

THE NATIONAL REALM

A casual reading of the Scriptures is sufficient to show us how prayer is associated with communal, national, and international affairs. Frank Laubach writes of "prayer minutemen—a minute a day—to flash thousands of instantaneous prayers at people far and near."

Kings are found praying for themselves, for the people they rule, and for their enemies. Kings, and all in authority, are to be prayed for. (See Ezra 6:10; Jeremiah 29:7; 1 Timothy 2:2.) If ever our rulers needed the prayers of God's people and needed to pray for themselves, it is now. How confused they are! How impotent they are to solve the gigantic international problems facing them. The United Nations Assembly is bankrupt of ideas for a distressed world. Any ideas they may have for world peace they are utterly unable to carry out. This topsy-turvy world certainly needs our prayers.

Hosea gave us a pattern of national prayer, but he suggested the utter futility of such prayer if it is not followed by national righteousness and the intent to do God's will. (See Hosea 6:1–3.)

Two or three years ago, *Life* magazine carried a remarkable editorial on "Why Men Pray," from which we culled the following paragraphs:

During an impasse at the Constitutional Convention in June 1787, Benjamin Franklin addressed the chairman (George Washington) as follows: "The small progress we have made…is, methinks, a melancholy proof of the imperfection of the human understanding…. I have lived, sir, a long time; and the longer I live, the more convincing proofs I see of this truth, that God governs in the affairs of men. And if a sparrow cannot fall to the ground without His notice, is it probable that an empire can rise without His aid? We have been assured, sir, in the Sacred Writings, that 'except the Lord build the house, they labor in vain that build it.' I firmly believe this; and I also believe that, without His concurring aid, we shall succeed in this political building no better than the builders of Babel." Franklin then moved that daily prayers be offered before the Assembly again got down to business. The motion was lost, but not because these men did not believe in prayer. To avoid sectarian controversy, and for other practical reasons, they preferred to pray in private. But they prayed.

There is no human calculus of the effectiveness of prayer. Today, Congress opens every session with a prayer. Its sessions may be no very persuasive testimonials to the practice, but perhaps that only means that too few congressmen really pray. Judging by the large number of homes in which grace is said at meals, the habit of prayer is probably commoner among average Americans than their leaders sometimes suppose. At the United Nations sessions, there are no prayers at all. Granted the problem of inter-faith etiquette, can anyone think prayers are not needed there?

CHAPTER 10

THE AGONY OF PRAYER

Few of us know much about wrestling in prayer. We find prayer pleasing and profitable but not painful. It is an easy exercise, never exhausting. We rejoice over the access prayer affords, but we are strangers to its agony. Prayer may take up a little of our time, but we never lose any blood, sweat, or tears over it.

At the outset of this aspect of our meditation, let it be noted that God does not expect us to agonize over those things we need. All we have to do is simply to ask, lovingly and truthfully. Desperation, shouting, and frenzy are not necessary when we come as children to our heavenly Father for the necessities of life. He is loving, kind, generous, and more willing to bless than we are to be blessed. *"He giveth to all men liberally, and upbraideth not"* (James 1:5). As the omniscient One, He knows all about our needs; and without coercion, without loud and much speaking, He will undertake to meet them.

There are times, however, when prayer is an agony. Our Lord, in Gethsemane, agonized in prayer. (See Matthew 26:36–46; Mark 14:32–42; Luke 22:39–46.) His supplications were sometimes saturated with anguish and tears. There were occasions when, as He prayed, He groaned in spirit. When He faced the powers of darkness, the hardness of men, and the weakness of the flesh, prayer was more than communion to Christ; it was a grim conflict. The Holy Spirit is described as groaning in prayer.

The word *strive*, which Paul often used in connection with prayer, is closely related in the Greek to our English term *agonize*.

Paul desired the saints of Rome to *"strive together with me in your prayers to God for me"* (Romans 15:30). Facing fierce satanic opposition in Asia, crushed and despairing even of life, Paul sought the tense, wrestling prayers of those who loved him in the Lord. And such prayers prevailed on his behalf. Paul wanted God's children, on whose prayers he relied, to labor with him in prayer for three things: *"That I might be delivered from them that do not believe"* (Romans 15:31); *"that my service which I have for Jerusalem may be accepted"* (verse 31); and *"that I may come unto you with joy by the will of God"* (verse 32).

Paul used the same expression about Epaphras, who was *"always **labouring** fervently for you in prayers, that ye may stand perfect and complete in all the will of God"* (Colossians 4:12, emphasis added). Writing to the Colossians, Paul reminded them of his spiritual burden and anguish on their behalf: *"I would that ye knew what **great conflict** I have for you, and for them at Laodicea, and for as many as have not seen my face in the flesh"* (Colossians 2:1, emphasis added).

The mightiest prayer warriors through the ages have been those who experienced something of the agony of Christ and of Paul in prayer. Theirs was the determination of the patriarch of old who, as he wrestled, cried, *"I will not let thee go, except thou bless me"* (Genesis 32:26).

John Fletcher stained the walls of his room by the breath of his frequent, earnest prayers.

John Welch, whose wife complained when she found him prostrate in prayer, replied, "O woman, I have the souls of three thousand to answer for, and I know not how it is with many of them!"

Henry Martyn lamented that "want of private devotional reading and shortness of prayer through incessant sermon-making had produced much strangeness between God and his soul," yet was characterized by much fervor in prayer.

The preacher Edward Payson, we are told by his biographer, wore the hardwood boards into groves where his knees pressed so often and so long in ardent and persevering prayer.

William Bramwell, the famous English Methodist preacher, would often spend as many as four hours agonizing in a single session of prayer. No wonder he went over his circuit as a flame of fire.

John Wesley also knew something of hell-shaking prayers. "Give me one hundred preachers who fear nothing but sin and desire nothing but God, and I care not a straw whether they be clergymen or laymen; such alone will shake the gates of hell and set up the kingdom of heaven on earth. God does nothing but in answer to prayer."

In his heart-warming volume *Prayer*, Ole Hallesby has two telling chapters entitled "Wrestling in Prayer," parts one and two, in which he expounded on the kind of prayer involving anguish and suffering. He asks, "Why should our prayer life be a constantly flowing source of anguish?" Then follow thirty-two pages of some of the most remarkable material ever written on the nature and need of agonizing prayer.

A strenuous, powerful prayer life becomes the target of satanic antagonism. The devil knows the effect of such praying upon his kingdom, and he mobilizes everything that he can commandeer in order to destroy wrestling prayers. Then, as Dr. Hallesby notes, the devil "has an excellent confederate in our bosoms: our old Adam." And how this old nature rebels against any form of prayer, especially the form of praying we are now considering. Our carnal nature is full of enmity toward God and hates everything related to the spiritual life. Thus, with the devil and the flesh against us, victory over principalities, powers, and the spiritual hosts of wickedness requires the wrestling in prayer that Paul not only wrote of but also experienced. (See Ephesians 6:12.)

Let these weighty words of Hallesby sink into your mind: "Everyone who is experienced in prayer knows that to listen quietly and humbly for what the Spirit of prayer says requires continued and powerful wrestling. It requires wrestling in the very first place, in order to hear and obey the Spirit's admonitions to prayer. Indeed, it involves both wrestling and watching, as Jesus said in Mark 13:38, because the spirit is willing to pray, but the flesh is weak." Further, "a struggle is involved in listening to what the Spirit has to say also while we pray."

Then, Hallesby points out, and rightly so, that this kind of praying is often misunderstood. "It has been conceived of as a struggle in prayer against God, the thought being that God withholds His gifts as long as possible," and they have to be wrung from Him. Such a conception of "wrestling in prayer is pagan and not Christian." Our bountiful God needs no persuasion to meet His children's needs. Our striving is a struggle, not with God, but with the devil and ourselves. Satanic hostility, in addition to our own selfishness, slothfulness, lethargy, and ignorance concerning the true import of prayer, all alike demand striving, persevering prayer—prayer that faints not but continues steadfast until victory is won.

In linking fasting to prayer, Jesus introduced His disciples to the great struggle connected with such a privileged exercise. (See Mark 9:29.) The New Testament clearly teaches that fasting is related to fierce temptations, to the making of a decision or choice, and to the planning and carrying out of very difficult tasks as we face great and mighty acts. Such fasting is necessary so the believing person of prayer can mediate the accession of needed wisdom, guidance, and power from God. "Fasting," says Hallesby, "helps to give us that inner sense of spiritual penetration, by means of which we can discern clearly that for which the Spirit of prayer would have us pray in exceptionally difficult circumstances."

The distressed, confused plight of the world; the low spiritual condition of the church; the carnality and unspirituality of the average professing Christian; the multitudes dying in heathen darkness—all these demand that we bestir ourselves from ignorance or distaste of wrestling prayer. Prayers that shake heaven, confound hell, and compel the world to turn to God are not the short, heartless, insipid prayers we are content with now. They must be prayers motivated by the heartbeat of God and the passion and compassion of Calvary. They must approximate, in some measure, to the bloodstained, tear-soaked prayers of Him to whom prayer was a wrestling as well as an act of worship.

CHAPTER 11

THE POWER OF PRAYER

In his impressive volume *Reality of the Spiritual World*, Thomas Kelly asked, "Is there a giant circle of prayer, such that prayer may originate in God and swing down into us and back up into Himself?" How grateful we are that there is such a "giant circle of prayer." Both the Bible and history testify to the glorious possibilities of God-inspired prayer. There is no limit to what God is able to accomplish in response to those who know how to storm heaven. Miriam exclaimed, "*Sing ye to the* Lord, *for he hath triumphed gloriously*" (Exodus 15:21). How true this is!

The prayers of the righteous have helped to shape the history of the world. In prayer, men grasp the hand that controls all things. With the exercise of prayer, contact is made with the Creator of the ends of the earth. This is why the words of the poet William Cowper are true: "Satan trembles when he sees the weakest saint upon his knees."

If, however, we are not mighty in prayer, and we do not believe that prayer is the greatest spiritual asset, albeit an unused asset, in the world, then the power of heaven will never be released through our lives. If anyone is cognizant of the power of prayer, it is the devil. That is why he strives in every possible way to weaken our prayer aspirations and activities. Or, to rephrase Cowper's verse, "Satan chuckles when he sees the Christian sleeping on his knees."

While the question "Does God answer prayer?" is one of perennial interest, we have no need to prove what He does. It has been computed that out of six hundred sixty-seven biblical prayers for specific needs, there are four hundred fifty-four traceable answers. The Psalms carry numerous allusions to the fact of the power of prayer. Joshua's testimony (see Joshua 23:14), and also that of Solomon (see 1 Kings 8:23–24, 56), has been abundantly verified by the saints of every age.

> Pray, for God in heaven hears;
> Pray, for prayer will move the spheres;
> Pray, for earth hath many a need;
> Pray, for prayer is vital deed;
> Pray, for every prayer is gold;
> Pray, for prayer is joy untold;
> Pray, for praying leads to peace;
> Pray, for praying gives release;
> Pray, for prayer well pays its cost;
> Pray, for prayer is never lost.

Scattered throughout the previous pages of this volume are evidences that prayer is the mightiest force in the world. Let us now try to summarize how this dynamic agency has operated in the lives of many of the saints of God, for whom, as they prayed, God performed. The spiritual giants who have shaken the kingdom of darkness have been men and women of effectual prayer. They did not spend too much of their time studying prayer; they simply prayed. Across the pages of Scripture and church history, we trace the records of those who, in bold, holy faith, pleaded with God and were heard in that they feared.

Prayer has produced marvelous results in the lives of multitudes. When they laid hold of God, He laid hold of them, and something happened. What a wealth of testimony they have left us as to the power of prayer! How convincing are their answers to prayer! They came boldly to the throne of grace and were not sent empty away:

- Abraham prayed long for a son—Isaac came.
- Eliezer prayed for guidance—Rebekah appeared.
- Jacob prayed—his brother's attitude was changed.
- Moses prayed—heaven's wrath was subdued.
- Joshua prayed—Achan was discovered and Ai destroyed.
- Hannah prayed—Samuel was given to her.
- Elijah prayed—the heavens were shut and opened.
- Elisha prayed—drought came; a dead child lived again.
- David prayed—Ahithophel the traitor hanged himself.
- Jehoshaphat prayed—his enemies were routed.
- Hezekiah prayed—185,000 Assyrians were slain.
- Daniel prayed—archangels were set in motion.

True prayer releases divine forces and restrains evil forces:

- Jesus prayed—the pillars of the church were chosen.
- The disciples prayed—Pentecost brought the Holy Spirit.
- The early church prayed—Peter was liberated from prison.
- Savonarola prayed—a city was won for God.
- Martin Luther prayed—God brought reformation to the church.
- John Knox prayed—tyrants were terrified, and Scotland was blessed.
- George Whitefield prayed—a thousand souls were saved in one day.
- George Fox prayed—the Quaker movement was born.
- George Müller prayed—hungry orphans were fed.
- Hudson Taylor prayed—inland China was evangelized.
- Ashley S. Johnson prayed—his poor boys had a Bible college.

On we could go, citing thousands of witnesses, all proving the lengths to which God will go when men and women are prepared to lay hold of Him in prayer, refusing to let go until He blesses them. The consistent witnesses of Christian saints agree that prayer is the highest resource of the soul. Subjected to trials, sorrows, failures, and sin, they yet experienced the transforming power of prayer. Foes, adverse circumstances, weaknesses, attitudes—all were conquered as deep called unto deep.

> Lord, what a change within us one short hour
> Spent in Thy presence will prevail to make;
> What heavy burdens from our bosoms take,
> What parched fields refresh as with a shower!
> We kneel, and all about us seems to lower;
> We rise, and all, the distant and the near,
> Stands forth in sunny outline, brave and clear;
> We kneel, how weak; we rise, how full of power.
> Why should we ever weak or heartless be,
> Why are we ever overborne with care,
> Anxious or troubled, when with us is prayer,
> And joy, and strength, and courage are with Thee?[27]

We ought always to pray and not to faint, since prayer's mighty power avails for the needs of the body, covers the cares of the home; enables us to face heavy responsibilities; empowers for Christian service; triumphs over hostile, satanic forces; and changes circumstances, sinners, and saints.

May we be named among God's prayer warriors, able to subdue kingdoms, stop the mouths of lions, and put to flight the enemies of God. As war drums continue to beat, we have so much to pray for. Prayer can prevail for our rulers, our generals, our forces, our chaplains, the bereaved, the prisoners of war, the

27. Richard C. Trench, "Lord, What a Change Within Us," 1856.

multitudes living in suspense, and ourselves. That all-necessary faith, hope, and courage may be ours as we await the coming of the Bridegroom.

Pray, always pray; the Holy Spirit pleads
Within thee all thy daily, hourly needs.

Pray, always pray; beneath sin's heaviest load
Prayer sees the blood from Jesus' side that flowed.

Pray, always pray; though weary, faint, and alone,
Prayer nestles by the Father's sheltering throne.

Pray, always pray; amid the world's turmoil
Prayer keeps the heart at rest, and nerves for toil.

Pray, always pray; if joys thy pathway throng,
Prayer strikes the harp, and sings the angels' song.

Pray, always pray; if loved ones pass the veil,
Prayer drinks with them of springs that cannot fail.

All earthly things with earth shall fade away;
Prayer grasps eternity; pray, always pray.[28]

Prayer is an instrument of God whereby He liberates power in the realms of nature and of grace on our behalf. We have, for example, the following proofs of the power of prayer:

1. Christ's interpretation of God as the all-sovereign One. He taught the personality of God as the heavenly Father who loves and cares.

2. God is not a prisoner in His own world, bound by laws of His own creation. He is the God of the impossible.

3. The finished work of Christ made possible access and boldness of approach to God. Redemption ground means privilege.

28. E. H. Bickersteth, "Pray, Always Pray, the Holy Spirit Pleads," 1885.

4. The Holy Spirit, as the Spirit of power, is the saint's Enabler and Inspirer as he intercedes for others.

5. The vast family of God, with varied experiences, trustworthy in character, mighty through God to the pulling down of strongholds, has left records that cannot be disputed. They were not deceived, and their declared achievements by prayer are not based upon falsehood.

6. Rich Bible promises encourage us to lay hold on God, and prove how willing and ready He is to accomplish whatever we ask of Him, so long as what we plead for is in accordance with His blessed will.

Do we know how to pray in such a way as to receive answers? Do we deem the silence of God in response to our prayers as one of the most dreadful things we could experience? Do we believe that prayer is a field which is twice reaped, in that it can...

1. *Sanctify the suppliant.* It purifies the life. Charles Spurgeon said, "Praying will either make a man leave off sinning, or else sinning will make a man leave off praying." Praying, we grow in grace. Prayer stretches the sinews of the soul and hardens its muscles. Prayer creates an inward peace nothing can disturb.

2. *Glorify the suppliant.* Secret prayer brings open reward. (See Matthew 6:6.) As the life becomes the channel through which God's power is released, the person of prayer, shunning all self-glorification, ascribes all glory to God, since all power is His.

The old ship captain John Newton taught us how to sing:

My soul ask what thou wilt,
Thou canst not be too bold;
Since His own blood for thee was spilt,
What else can He withhold?

Beyond thine utmost wants,
His love and pow'r can bless;
To praying souls He always grants,
More than they can express.[29]

---

29. John Newton, "Behold the Throne of Grace," 1779.

CHAPTER 12

THE PROBLEMS OF PRAYER

Although the art of simplicity is the heart of prayer, prayer yet carries difficulties and problems that some minds find hard to cope with. There are those who seem to be baffled by the exercise, laws, and results of prayer. Because we deem this to be a most important and intensely practical aspect of our meditation, let us seek to clarify many prayer problems.

THE PROBLEM OF NATURAL ORDER

Sophisticated men, such as Kant, the philosopher, think it "absurd and presumptuous" to ask favors of God. It is viewed as arrogance to ask God to alter His cosmic plans for ourselves or others. The universe is viewed as a "closed system, fixed unalterably by natural law, a system in which nothing but foregone conclusions can happen." Thus, prayer is contrary to the reign of law in nature. It is impertinence to expect that the through traffic on the highways of the laws of nature can be sidetracked for a "local train" carrying our puny petitions.

With the advance of modern science, however, such a problem is purely artificial. The universe is now an open one. Laws still reign within the universe, but amid and through these laws are open possibilities, open to initiative and creative faith. Natural law used to say that nothing heavier than air could remain aloft. Now, bombers weighing tons fly through the air. Atomic and electric energy also prove how man is able to utilize natural laws.

That renowned jurist, Oliver Wendell Holmes, said, "The mode in which the inevitable comes to pass is through effort." The witness of Scripture and history is that if God's plans are inevitable, man's voluntary prayers can still be part of the effort on which He counts to fulfill them. It is upon this paradox that our Christian faith is built. Those who believe in the reality, possibilities, and power of prayer worship a God who knows and foresees all, yet "whose service is perfect freedom." To them, God is greater than all the laws He created, and He can command any one of them to obey His will on behalf of His redeemed children.

THE PROBLEM OF WRONG APPROACH

Scripture is plain on the point that God both hears and answers prayer. His ear is never heavy that it cannot hear the right kind of petition. (See Isaiah 59:1.) We are urged to pray at all times, in all places, and for all needs. It is essential to believe that God "*is a rewarder of them that diligently seek him*" (Hebrews 11:6). The scope of His promise is...

1. without limit of place: "*Pray every where*" (2 Timothy 2:8).

2. without limit of time: "*Always*" (Luke 18:1).

3. without limit of subject: "*In every thing*" (Philippians 4:6). (See also Matthew 21:22; John 16:23.)

Whether our requirements are sacred or secular, spiritual or material, God waits to grant us those things we desire of Him. He assures us of His constant care and concern, and that...

There is no place where earth's sorrows
Are more felt than up in heaven.[30]

---

30. Frederick W. Faber, "There's a Wideness in God's Mercy," 1854.

But, while all this is so, God answers our prayers only when they are presented in the way of His appointing and according to His superior intelligence. Answered prayer, then, depends on the right approach to the throne of grace. Prayer will never be sound and normal unless we pray aright. Prayer has its laws, which must be known and obeyed.

Ole Hallesby enlarged on some of the errors to guard against if prayer would be effective in our lives. Readers are directed to his book *Prayer* and a chapter entitled "Difficulties in Prayer." One of these errors concerns the idea that we must help God to fulfill our petitions. All God asks of us is to pray. He Himself carries the responsibilities of hearing and fulfilling.

Neither do we have to pray in order to make God kind and good to answer our prayer. God is ever good, and He grants us what we need of His own accord. He is love, and the essence of love is to give. Prayer, then, is "not for the purpose of making God good or generous. He is that from all Eternity.... Prayer has one function, and that is to answer 'Yes' when He knocks, to open the soul and give Him the opportunity to bring us the answer."

We also pray amiss when we make use of prayer for the purpose of commanding God to do our bidding. Some arrogant, demanding prayers are an insult to the Almighty. He is not an inferior to whom orders are to be issued. Wrote Hallesby, "God has not given us His promises and the privilege of prayer in order that we might use them to pound a demanding fist upon the table before God and compel Him to do what we ask." We violate the governing laws of prayer if we think we have to bring our influence to bear upon Him and thereby compel Him to answer us.

A further misuse of prayer is that of trying to make use of God for our own personal advantage and enjoyment. Selfishness, even in a Christian, knows no bounds. The carnal nature desires everything for itself. We are given an example of a misused request in Matthew 20:20–23, when the mother of Zebedee's children asked

Jesus that her two sons *"may sit, the one on thy right hand, and the other on the left, in thy kingdom"* (verse 21). Selfish prayers have been humorously ridiculed in this little poem:

> Lord bless me and my wife,
> My son, Tom, and his wife,
> Us four—
> No more. Amen!

Prayer in the name of Jesus Christ our Lord involves correspondence with His will and harmony with His wishes. (See Acts 19:13–16.) In the field of radio, the transmitting and receiving sets must be attuned. So with prayer; there must be sympathy with the Lord's plans and purposes. Presenting our petitions in Christ's name is equivalent to coming before God with Christ's authority. The power of prayer depends upon the right use of the name that is above every other name. Bearing His name implies likeness to His character. Employment of His name means identity of interests—union with Christ in His will and ways. (See John 15:16; 16:23–26.)

Hallesby remarked that "to pray in the name of Jesus is, in all likelihood, the deepest mystery in prayer.... Scripture speaks of the *'mystery of Christ'* (Ephesians 3:4). The name of Jesus is the greatest mystery in heaven and on earth. In heaven, this mystery is known; on earth, it is unknown to most people. No one can fathom it fully....To pray in the name of Jesus is the real element of prayer in our prayers. It is the helpless soul's helpless look unto a gracious Friend. The wonderful results which attend prayer of this kind can be accounted for only by the fact that we have opened the door unto Jesus and given Him access to our helplessness."

THE "IF" OF FAITH

Jesus answered and said unto them, Verily I say unto you, If ye have faith, and doubt not, ye shall not only do this which is

> *done to the fig tree, but also if ye shall say unto this mountain,*
> *Be thou removed, and be thou cast into the sea; it shall be*
> *done. And all things, whatsoever ye shall ask in prayer, believ-*
> *ing, ye shall receive.*   (Matthew 21:21–22)

As faith is the only means of communication with the invisible God, it is essential to the offering and answering of prayer. (See Hebrews 11:6; James 1:6–7.) In prayer, *"all things are possible to him that believeth"* (Mark 9:23). Great faith results in great blessing. (See Matthew 8:10, 13; 15:28.) While prayer is the key to all the treasures of heaven, faith is the hand using that key. Our Lord would have us realize the necessity of possessing the kind of faith able to believe that God has answered our prayers before the actual reception of the blessings sought. (See Mark 11:14, 20, 23–24; John 11:41). Too many of us fail in our prayer lives because of a lack of faith.

The threadbare story of the minister calling for a day of prayer for rain to relieve the drought afflicting the community comes to mind. A Sunday was chosen for such a day, and what a day is was! Brilliant sunshine, with not a cloud on the horizon. A maiden turned up on the sunny Sunday with an umbrella under her arm to pray for rain. Several members chided the girl for bringing an umbrella to church on such a bright, cloudless day. "Well," she said, "we are told to come and pray for rain, and we must believe that God will send it." Ere the service was over, we are told, the rain appeared, and Mary went home under her umbrella, the happiest church member that day. Others got soaked, but she reached home dry. Prayer had been mixed with faith.

THE "IF" OF ABIDING

> *If ye abide in me and my words abide in you, ye shall ask what*
> *ye will, and it shall be done unto you.*   (John 15:7)

Habitual obedience to all of God's commands is also bound up with effective prayer. How useless it is to pray if we refuse to do all the Lord requires of us! Prayer can be acceptable to Him only as it ascends from an obedient heart. (See Proverbs 1:24–31; 28:8; Zechariah 7:13; 1 John 3:22.) "Our obedience," says William Proctor, "does not in itself merit an answer to our prayer, but it is a test of our fitness to receive it, and an indispensable qualification for our obtaining our petitions."

We recognize the fact that we have a judicial standing in Christ that nothing can affect. Union with Him can never be severed, but communion can. Thus, to abide in Christ means to have no known, willfully indulged sin to break communion with Him. Power in prayer is dependent upon such unbroken fellowship with Christ. (See Isaiah 59:1–2.)

> I am the Lord's! Yet teach me all it meaneth,
> All it involves of love and loyalty,
> Of holy service, absolute surrender,
> And unreserved obedience unto Thee.[31]

It will be observed that there is a twofold condition attached to prayer in our Lord's teaching. (See John 14:1–14). We must abide in Him and have His words abiding in us. The latter means more than having verses in our memory. We must meditate on Christ's words until they become part and parcel of our lives. It is only then that they strengthen us by giving our faith its warrant and its plea.

THE "IF" OF GOD'S WILL

And this is the confidence that we have in him, that if we ask any thing according to his will, he heareth us; and if we know

---

31. Lucy Ann Bennett, "I Am the Lord's! O Joy Beyond Expression," date unknown.

that he hear us, whatsoever we ask, we know that we have the petitions that we desired of him. (1 John 5:14–15)

John, in very simple, understandable language, assured us that all prayers that are according to God's will are sure of being heard and answered. The sequence is clear: "*If we ask any thing according to His will, he heareth us.*" Harmony with God's will, then, is not only an essential stipulation but also a necessary safeguard to our freedom in prayer. Christ's prayers ever were offered in full submission to the will of His Father. (See Matthew 25:39, 42; John 12:27, 29.) Alas, our own prayers are often marred by petulant self-will! We do not pray in the line of God's will but in the line of our own wills.

The confidence John spoke of is not associated with the obtaining of specific things asked for but the obtaining of answers in accordance with God's perfect wisdom and infinite love.

A difficulty confronting many is the question "What is the will of God?" Is it something secret? If so, then we can never have the confidence of asking which John spoke about. How can we know we are praying according to His will? Such a will is revealed in a threefold way:

1. *By the Word.* The broad principles of God's will are not to be found in isolated texts but in the Scriptures as a whole.

2. *By the Holy Spirit.* As a member of the Godhead, He knows the will of God and is cognizant of all that concerns Christ. If prayerfully depended upon, the Spirit will enable us to discern between the divine will and our own will and feelings.

3. *By circumstances._*Sanctified common sense is not only in deciding what is or is not of God. Discovering His will, we must seek grace and strength to fulfill it.

THE "IF" OF AGREEMENT

Again I say unto you, That if two of you shall agree on earth as touching any thing that they shall ask, it shall be done for them of my Father which is in heaven. For where two or three are gathered together in my name, there am I in the midst of them. (Matthew 18:19–20)

In this passage, our Lord taught His own the right approach to God in the matter of united prayer. Burgess and Lovelace give us this serviceable outline:

1. *Why united prayer succeeds and is powerful*: It recognizes our common membership of God's family. It realizes our common membership of Christ's body.

2. *When united prayer succeeds*: The principle of united consent: *"…if two of you shall agree."* The presence of the unseen Christ: *"I in the midst…."*

3. *What united prayer secures*: It deepens our mutual fellowship. It strengthens our personal faith. It increases our love and devotion to the Master. It alters the course of history because history is "His story."

THE PROBLEM OF HINDRANCES

Cowper's expressive hymn commences with the lines:

What various hindrances we meet
In coming to a mercy seat;
Yet who that knows the worth of prayer,
But wishes to be often there?[32]

Hindrances to prayer are many and manifold, external and internal. Satan, knowing that prayer is the arena of conflict and

32. William Cowper, "What Various Hindrances We Meet," 1779.

victory for the believer, uses all his art to destroy the effectiveness of prayer. He knows how to use outward circumstances and interruptions, apathy, straying thoughts, and indolence within for the weakening of the cable heavenward.

There are times when circumstances make it hard to pray. Job found this to be so when he lost his dear ones—his house, his wealth, his health. *"Behold, I cry out of wrong, but I am not heard"* (Job 19:7). Jeremiah, when the sorrows of captive Zion were overwhelming his compassionate soul, found it hard to pray. (See Lamentations 2:4, 7; 3:44.) His persevering prayers were ultimately victorious, however, and in the prophet's dark hour, God was his light.

Are you sitting in the shadows without much time for prayer and meditation? Are your circumstances "ganging up" on you until it seems as if you lift up your hands into empty space? Is yours the following complaint?

> Lord, I am tired. I can bring to Thee
> Only a heavy weight of tiredness.
> I kneel, but all my mind's a vacancy,
> And conscious only of its weakness—
> Can it be prayer, this dragging dreariness?

No, such dragging dreariness is not conducive to effectual prayer.

Interruptions form another external hindrance to prayer. We retire to pray, but the children cry, the telephone rings, the doorbell clangs, and tradesmen call. The more intent we are on concentrated prayer, the more interruptions seem to overtake us. Well, as Samuel Zwemer pointed out, we can be patient with such interruptions and make them stepping-stones instead of stumbling blocks in the way of prayer, if only we will study the example of Jesus. How wonderful He was at making every interruption an opportunity for the exercise of His healing power or His comforting words! (See Mark 6:34, 46.)

Forced to relinquish our posture in prayer, we can remain in the spirit of prayer and, as we go to the phone or the door, pray for those who unknowingly interrupted the blessed hour of prayer. If you are interrupted, let the interruption be not an irritation but an interpretation. The season of prayer will be richer for the mastery of interruption. Evangelize the inevitable.

Other hindrances making true prayer difficult or impossible are indolence, pride, selfishness, formality, idols of the heart, jealousy, and ruptured relationship. The book of Daniel makes it clear that there are determined satanic hindrances to prayer. All obstacles, however, are not long in vanishing if we have more purpose in prayer and learn how to pray in the Spirit.

THE PROBLEM OF DELAYED ANSWERS

Some prayers appear to pass unanswered. But their answers are not denied—only delayed. We are apt to misjudge the seemingly slow movements of God. In our rash haste, we want immediate answers. We have to learn with Mary and Martha, however, that His delays are not denials. (See John 11:6.) The mills of God may appear to grind slowly, but they grind exceedingly sure. It has been said that "when our prayers make long voyages, they come back laden with richer cargoes of blessing;" and "when God keeps us waiting for an answer, He gives liberal interest for the interval." The parables of the selfish neighbor and the unjust judge teach us to persevere in prayer. (See Luke 18:4.) There may be delays indicating that God does not care. Jesus was silent when faced by the Phoenician woman; "*He answered her not a word*" (Matthew 5:23). But to the chagrin of the disciples, the needy woman continued her intercession until she got what she wanted. (See Matthew 15:21–29; 1 Peter 1:7.)

Delayed answers to our prayers are also profitable in that they cause us to search our hearts to make sure that the cause of divine silence is not in ourselves. Monica's prayers for the salvation of her much-loved son, Augustine, were delayed but not denied. Ultimately, God answered that mother's cry, and her gifted son was saved and became one of the choice saints of the church. *"Blessed are all they that wait for him"* (Isaiah 30:18). Often, delays are for our greater benefit. We are not always ready to receive the gifts we seek. Someone has said, "We want to pluck our mercies green, but God waits until they are ripe."

It may seem as a triumph of faith when answers come swiftly on the heels of our prayers, but delays make for discipline. Feverish faith is weak and must be taught to wait. Often, we intercede for unsaved relatives, yet no answer comes. We come to realize that we must wrestle like Jacob, pant like David, hope like Elijah, persist like Bartimaeus, and weep like Jeremiah and Jesus before answers appear.

Moses prayed to go into Canaan, but his request to enter the Promised Land seemed to be denied. (See Deuteronomy 3:23, 29.) He died at Pisgah, and Israel entered Canaan without their leader. Yet some fifteen hundred years later, the prayer of Moses was answered, and we find him on the Mount of Transfiguration. (See Matthew 17:1–9; Mark 9:2–8; Luke 9:28–36.)

Elijah was mighty in prayer, and God answered all his prayers, save for one. Under the juniper tree, suffering from mental and physical reaction, the prophet prayed that he might die. It was a mercy that God did not take him at his word. The prayers of a despondent, fretful, overtired saint are seldom valid. Elijah went to heaven in a more glorious way than that of death.

David wanted to build the house of God. His heart was set on such a task, and he prayed much about it. God praised him for wanting to do so but forbade his execution of the task. His prayers were answered in Solomon's day.

The demon-possessed man, after the miracle of his healing, prayed that he might accompany Jesus to witness of His grace, but he was sent home to testify among his relatives and friends. (See Luke 8:38.)

Unanswered yet?
The prayers your lips have pleaded
In agony of heart these many years?
Does faith begin to fail, is hope departing,
And think you all in vain those falling tears?
Say not the Father hath not heard your prayer:
You shall have your desire, sometime, somewhere.[33]

If your sincere prayer appears to pass unanswered, you must not be weary in well-doing. All Spirit-inspired prayers are answered in God's good time. In patience, we must possess our souls.

THE PROBLEM OF DIFFERENT ANSWERS

If our prayers are not answered in *kind*, they are answered in *kindness*. With His infinite wisdom, God knows that which is best for His children, and He answers their petitions according to His own intelligence.

The ambitious request of James and John was answered in a way they did not expect. Because they were cousins of our Lord and members of the inner circle, they thought a favor was due them. Suffering for Christ is the prelude to reigning with Him. (See Mark 10:35–40; Romans 8:17; 2 Timothy 2:12.) James was the first apostle to suffer martyrdom; John, the last.

33. Charles D. Tillman, "Unanswered Yet," 1894.

Paul prayed for the removal of his thorn. Fervently, and thrice over, he presented his petition, and God answered—not by removing the burden, but by granting Paul sufficient grace to carry it. (See 2 Corinthians 12:7–10.) The messenger of Satan sent to buffet the apostle became the minister of God to bless him, enabling him *"to glory in my infirmities, that the power of Christ may rest upon me"* (2 Corinthians 12:9). God gave His servant a larger answer to his prayer. Paul's experience teaches us the patience of unanswered prayer and the victory of faith. Consider this anonymous "Confederate Soldier's Prayer":

I asked God for strength, that I might achieve;
I was made weak, that I might learn humbly to obey.
I asked for health, that I might do greater things;
I was given infirmity, that I might do better things.
I asked for riches, that I might be happy;
I was given poverty, that I might be wise.
I asked for power, that I might have the praise of men;
I was given weakness, that I might feel the need of God.
I asked for all things, that I might enjoy life;
I was given life, that I might enjoy all things.
I got nothing that I asked for, but everything I hoped for.
Almost despite myself, my unspoken prayers were
answered.
I am among all men most richly blessed.

The most agonized petition Jesus ever made was not immediately granted. *"Abba, Father,"* He cried in the garden, *"all things are possible unto thee; take away this cup from me: nevertheless not what I will, but what thou wilt"* (Mark 14:36). The cup was not taken away. Jesus was not saved from death. (See Hebrews 5:7.) An angel strengthened Him to drain the bitter cup of suffering. (See Luke 22:43.) Out He went to endure the cross and despise its shame (see Hebrews 12:2), that no Christian should ever feel abandoned by his Lord.

For every true believer, the prayer can ever arise:

> While withholding—Thou art giving
> In Thine own appointed way
> And while waiting we're receiving
> Blessings suited to our day.[34]

THE PROBLEM OF UNANSWERED PRAYERS

The problem of unanswered prayer is acute. We all feel it. Its mystery shrouds our faith at some time or another. We pray to God, but the heavens seem as brass. Distress and rebellion become ours. Can God be indifferent? Has He forgotten us or ceased to care? Our hearts protest with the psalmist, *"How long wilt thou forget me, O Lord? for ever? how long wilt thou hide thy face from me?"* (Psalm 13:1). *"This thou hast seen, O Lord: keep not silence"* (Psalm 35:22). But silence seems to reign, and we are perplexed.

Let us introduce this vexed problem by stating that there are prayers God must answer. Because the Christian is in a covenant of union and communion with God, He is bound to honor the same. Being redeemed, the person of prayer exercises the covenant privilege of prayer. The basis of his bold approach is the blood of the Redeemer. (See Hebrews 4:16; 10:19, 22.) The essence of prayer is found in a right relationship with God. If such a relationship is lacking, He is under no obligation to answer prayer.

Among the prayers which God must answer are prayers for...

+ deliverance from sin. *"Him that cometh to me I will in no wise cast out"* (John 6:37).

---

34. Jane Crewdson, "Lord, We Know That Thou Art Near Us," 1868.

+ holiness of life. *"This is the will of God, even your sanctification"* (1 Thessalonians 4:3).

+ the infilling of the Spirit. *"If ye then, being evil, know how to give good gifts unto your children: how much more shall your heavenly Father give the Holy Spirit to them that ask him?"* (Luke 11:13).

+ relief from physical and material needs, if such is His will. *"Call upon me in the day of trouble: I will deliver thee"* (Psalm 50:15).

+ the second advent. *"Even so, come, Lord Jesus"* (Revelation 22:20).

In the next place, there are prayers God will not answer. As we have already seen, there are laws and conditions attached to prayer. Unrestricted promises are hedged about with limitations. Unlimited invitations are surrounded with conditions we sometimes fail to observe. We are commanded to pray for all men, yet there are those whom we are forbidden to intercede for. (See Jeremiah 7:16; 1 John 5:15–16.) We ask and receive not, since the ear of God is closed to the suppliant. (See Lamentations 3:44.) Because prayer is the naked intent stretching out to God, our prayers must be clean, as well as our hearts.

Among prayers God cannot answer are prayers…

+ lacking sincerity and faith. (See Matthew 6:5, 7; Hebrews 11:6; James 1:6–7.)

+ substituting for action. (See Exodus 14:15; Joshua 7:7–13.)

+ inspired by carnal motives. (See James 4:2–3.)

+ framed to change God's decrees. (See Deuteronomy 3:23–27; Hebrews 1:1–4; Habakkuk 1:1–4.)

+ disregarding the revealed will of God. (See 1 Samuel 8:9–19.)

+ arising from an unclean heart. (See Psalm 66:18; Lamentations 3:8, 40–44.)

+ desirous of averting necessary chastisement. (See 2 Samuel 12:16–18; 2 Corinthians 12:7–9.)

+ seeking the recall of lost opportunities. (See Luke 13:25–28.)

+ accompanied by unconfessed sin. (See 1 John 1:8–10.)

+ fashioned out of meaningless and repetitious phrases. (See Matthew 6:7.)

+ offered in foolish pride and arrogance. (See Proverbs 8:13.)

+ prompted by selfish motives. (See Matthew 6:5; James 4:2–3.)

+ arising out of a heart full of ill will and hatred toward others. (See Matthew 5:24.)

The following lines by Annie Lind Woodworth are full of appeal:

UNANSWERED PRAYER

Unanswered, does your prayer remain
Though oft with tears you plead?
And watch and wait and wonder if
God does not care or heed?

Unanswered? Well, perhaps, dear heart,
You may have asked amiss;
Is it God's glory that you seek,
Or selfish avarice?

How often selfish motives form
A prayer God cannot grant;
None can deceive th'Omniscient One
With merely pious cant.

Oh, that we might all clearly see
That God will not be mocked;

Against impostors, the door
Of answered prayer is locked.

Deep in some recess of your heart,
Perhaps some stubborn sin
Forbids the righteous God to grant
The answer you would win.

Perchance an Achan, in the camp,
Bars answer to your prayer;
When He receives confessing grace,
Your answer will be there.

Upon the hindrances God throws
His searchlight, powerful, strong;
But how we squirm, and fain would think
We misconstrue the wrong.

Unanswered? Tested one, pray on—
God will allay each fear—
Give grace and courage to endure
Till answers shall appear.

A little more of suffering,
Of pain and tears for thee;
A little more of trustful prayers,
Then—answers thou shalt see.

Unanswered? No! For even now
God's hand is working out
A plan by which, eventually,
That hindrance He will rout.

Often, we receive not because we ask amiss. Ignorance as to God's requirements and the principles of prayer blocks the channel. This is why the specific ministry of the Spirit has been provided. In our prayer infirmity, He is the divine Helper. (See Romans 8:26–27.)

It remains to be said that while God does answer some of the prayers of the unconverted, He has not promised to do so. All promises of answered prayer are given to the regenerated children—to those in covenant relationship with Him as their heavenly Father.

Are you facing the problem of unanswered prayer? As far as you know, your heart is right in God's sight, your motives are pure, and your requests are legitimate enough, yet no answer comes. Do not cease to pray. God is silent in His love. (See Zephaniah 3:17.) Because of His inscrutable wisdom, He knows what is best for you. He has answers beyond your expected answers. When all the mysteries of life are unraveled, then you will praise Him for your unanswered prayers.

When fuller, perfect light is ours, we will understand that "No" was an answer, as well as "Yes." Often, we hear it said, "God didn't answer my prayer." But He did. He may not have given what was insisted upon, any more than we would give a child a serpent that looked like a fish because he begged for it, or a stone shaped like a piece of bread. (See Luke 11:15.) Yet He does answer in His own way, which is ever the best way. What we deem to be refusals are the only answers possible to His love, wisdom, and truth. A heathen poet wrote, "That Power above, who makes mankind His care, may bless us most when He rejects our prayer."

Many of our prayers, unanswered while we live, are fully answered after we cross the river of death. There are *"golden vials full of odours, which are the prayers of saints"* (Revelation 5:8), constantly remembered by God.

Mr. Badman's wife was deeply concerned over the lost estate of her husband, but John Bunyan made her to say, "Are my prayers lost? are they forgotten? are they thrown over the bar? No; they are hanged upon the horns of the golden altar, and I must have the benefit of them myself, that moment that I shall enter into the gates, in at which the righteous nation that keepeth truth shall enter.... My prayers are not lost; my tears are yet in God's bottle."

Yes, at daybreak, our hearts will confess:

> He answered prayer—not in the way I sought,
> Nor in the way that I had thought He ought;
> But in His own good way; and I could see
> He answered in the fashion best for me.

CHAPTER 13

THE INSPIRER OF PRAYER

Each Person of the blessed Trinity is related to the exercise of prayer. We have access to the Father, through the Son, by the Spirit. (See Ephesians 2:18.) In particular:

1. God the Father hears and answers prayer. (See Psalm 17:6; Matthew 7:11; Hebrews 11:6.) Graciously, He permits us to approach Him at all times.

2. God the Son presents our imperfect prayers and blends them with His perfect propitiation. (See Hebrews 7; Revelation 8:3.) He is our ladder, set up on earth, by which we ascend to the Father. He bridges both worlds. All prayers must be in His name. (See John 14:13–14.)

3. God the Spirit is the Inspirer of true prayer. (See Romans 8:26–27.) How dependent we are upon the Spirit as we come to pray! Often, we are inclined to ask what would be hurtful if granted. As Shakespeare wrote, "We, ignorant of ourselves, beg often our own harm." When we know not how to pray aright, the Spirit is at hand to prompt our prayers and purify our motives. (See James 4:3.)

The Scriptures teach that He is *"spirit of grace and of supplications"* (Zechariah 12:10) and is therefore the Source and Sphere of our prayers. (See Romans 8:14–27; Galatians 4:6–7; Ephesians 6:18; Jude 20.) We read, "He cries," and "we cry," suggesting, as Andrew Murray said, "a wonderful blending of the divine and human cooperation in prayer."

When the Spirit takes possession of the soul and becomes, essentially, the Spirit of intercession—and, as such, overcomes our infirmity in our not being able to pray aright—He is our aid in prayer, covering every outgoing of the mind and heart toward God, whether in the nature of supplication, confession, intercession, praise, or adoration. Without the Holy Spirit, our prayers are as lifeless as a body without a soul, as ineffective as an arrow without a bow. "The Spirit," as Norman Harrison stated, "is at once the guide of prayer and the guarantor of its success." Let us try to analyze the outstanding features of this mystic truth.

THE SPIRIT IS THE INSPIRER OF PRAYER

The divine Spirit first brings the soul into right relationship with God. The right and privilege of the children of God to pray become theirs. (See Galatians 4:6–7.) The desire and ability to pray are made possible by the Spirit. Sonship is the true starting point of all access to God. Fear, with its enslaving influence, is driven out, the spirit of adoption taking its place. The Spirit becomes the filial Spirit, whereby we cry, "Abba, Father!"

Spirit-inspired prayer is impossible without an *act of memory*, by which our sins and divine mercy are recalled. It is the function of the Spirit to bring all things to our remembrance.

There must be also an *act of the mind*. The Spirit enables us to choose our words and to express ourselves in fitting language. He can deliver from distraction and grant us definite concentration. The Spirit quickens the mind and the emotions. He prepares, possesses, and prompts the mind, so that we can continue in prayer. (See Luke 18:1; 1 Thessalonians 5:17.) The difference between *saying prayers* and *praying* is in having a Spirit-possessed mind. He teaches us to pray not by outward forms but by inward compulsion. As the Spirit of wisdom, He prevents us from uttering unwise petitions.

We must likewise know something of *the act of love*, which enables us to enter sympathetically into the needs of others. As the Spirit of love, He sheds abroad the love of God in our hearts. (See Ephesians 2:18; 6:18; Philippians 3:3.)

THE SPIRIT AROUSES THE SOUL TO A SENSE OF NEED

God's gracious Spirit opens to the child of God a vision of a new world of purity and power by revealing the contrast between the old, natural life and the new life in Christ. Norman Harrison indicated four things relating to the Spirit's help in prayer:

1. Its necessity: Our weakness and ignorance.

2. Its nature: He prays in us and for us.

3. Its assured acceptance: His mind, wrought in us, is known to God.

4. Its assured answer: He prays for us according to God's will.

Once within, the Spirit awakens desire for communion with God, to which we had been strangers. Through His illuminating grace and promptings, we are made conscious of our needs and how to pray aright about them. What we do not know, the Spirit knows! It is thusly that He works in our hearts, begetting earnest longings after those things well-pleasing to God. Prayer will never enable us to attain to deeper holiness of life unless it is prayer in the Spirit.

Paul's exhortation about praying in the Spirit goes down to the depths and includes more than an ordinary and coherent experience or expression in prayer. It refers to those unfathomed depths in man where there are feelings and yearnings so mysterious that our minds cannot give them definite form or correct articulation. In the obscure realm down in human personality, from which yearnings come, the Spirit moves with perfect familiarity and sympathizes with these mysterious longings for which there is no language but a sigh or a cry. *"He that searcheth the hearts knoweth what is the mind of the Spirit"* (Romans 8:27).

If we were all we should be, and could pray aright, there would be no need of the Spirit's help. But, because we are imperfect and beset with weakness and ignorance, the prayer ministry of the Spirit is constantly necessary.

Pray, always pray: the Holy Spirit pleads.
Within thee all thy daily, hourly needs.

THE SPIRIT INTERCEDES FOR US

Believers are blessed with two divine Intercessors: one in heaven; the other in the human heart. Twice over, the Spirit is referred to as our Intercessor. (See Romans 8:26–27.) The Lord Jesus Christ is in heaven, ever interceding for us. (See Hebrews 7:25.) He is our Advocate on high. (See Hebrews 9:24; 1 John 2:1.) The Spirit is within, prompting prayer; Christ is above, presenting our petition. The Spirit is "the chamber advocate," preparing our case; Christ is "the court advocate," presenting our case. Thus, as hymnist James Montgomery put it, we have a twofold plea: "Hear me, for Thy Spirit pleads; hear, for Jesus intercedes."

The Spirit prays *in*, as well as *with* and *for*, us. In some profound manner, His personality is identified with ours for the purpose of intercession. As God's free Spirit, He mingles with our spirits and thus makes our prayers His own, or, rather, creates them within our minds. As the Spirit of intercession, He exercises the function within us, just as Christ exercises His intercessory work about us in heaven. (See Romans 8:34.) Christ is our Paraclete on earth. The Spirit lays bare all the deep and hidden needs of the saint; Christ, in merit of His death and resurrection, pleads for the meeting of such needs.

> Prayer is not made by us alone:
> The Holy Spirit pleads,
> And Jesus, on the eternal throne,
> For sinners intercedes.[35]

Two features in connection with the groaning of the Spirit must be observed: These unutterable groanings are known and understood by God, and they are in accordance with the will of God, which is the keynote of all true intercession.

THE SPIRIT BESTOWS FULL ASSURANCE OF FAITH

What we seek in prayer, believing, we receive. Inspiring us to pray, the Spirit also produces a corresponding faith, so that true prayer becomes the prayer of faith, enabling us to ask believingly. (See Hebrews 10:22.) This assurance produces a clear recognition of God as the Source supplying all our needs. (See James 1:17.) Such assurance also unfolds the power and the willingness of God to bestow good things through His Son and by His Spirit. (See Ephesians 2:18.)

If we would guard ourselves from deadness and despondency in the inner chamber, then, as dear, saintly Andrew Murray told us:

1. We must firmly believe, as a divine reality, that the Spirit of God's Son, the Holy Spirit, is in us.

2. We must understand all the Spirit desires to accomplish in us. His work in prayer is closely connected with His other work.

---

35. James Montgomery, "Prayer Is the Soul's Sincere Desire," 1818.

3. We must recognize His claim to the full possession of our lives. As the soul has the whole body for its dwelling place and service, so the Holy Spirit must have our body and soul as His dwelling place, entirely under His control. Then, and then only, can He function as the Spirit of prayer!

ABOUT THE AUTHOR

When Dr. Herbert Lockyer (1886–1984) was first deciding on a career, he considered becoming an actor. Tall and well-spoken, he seemed a natural for the theater. But the Lord had something better in mind. Instead of the stage, God called Herbert to the pulpit, where, as a pastor, Bible teacher, and author of more than fifty books, he touched the hearts and lives of millions of people.

Dr. Lockyer held pastorates in Scotland and England for twenty-five years. As pastor of Leeds Road Baptist Church in Bradford, England, he became a leader in the Keswick Higher Life Movement, which emphasized the significance of living in the fullness of the Holy Spirit. This led to an invitation to speak at the Moody Bible Institute's fiftieth anniversary in 1936. His warm reception at that event led to his ministry in the United States. He received honorary degrees from both the Northwestern Evangelical Seminary and the International Academy in London.

In 1955, he returned to England, where he lived for many years. He then returned to the United States, where he spent the final years of his life in Colorado Springs, Colorado, with his son, the Rev. Herbert Lockyer Jr., a Presbyterian minister who became his editor.